369 Method to Manifest Abundance

Law of Attraction Guide for Beginners

Table of Contents

Introduction

Congratulations on purchasing: 369 Method to Manifest Abundance; Law of Attraction Guide for Beginners, and thank you for doing so.

The following chapters will discuss the law of attraction and how it works. Additionally, we will go over the law of vibrations and how it benefits your manifestations. Then once you know the basics, we will go over how science supports law of attraction. Finally, we will provide you with the information and tips to help you manifest the life you want.

There are many books on this subject you could have chosen. Thank you so much for picking this book! I made every effort to ensure this book provides you with all the information you need to start manifesting using the law of attraction and the 369 method to your benefit. Please enjoy!

Chapter 1: How My Conversation with the Universe Began

Like many people I've gone through hard times in my life; that I thought would never end. Due to circumstances out of my control I had to move, I lost my job, and everything seemed to be falling apart. Then, I learned about Rhonda Byrnes's book The Secret. A buddy of mine gave me a copy of the book to help me through the challenging period. However, I ended up putting it on my bookcase with the various other books I was putting off reading.

At that time, I found a new place to live and was offered a job that I was excited about. I was excited to get my life back on track. But, after a few months, my excitement quickly faded, and my workplace turned into an awful situation. My boss was cruel and egocentric then and manipulated people whenever he could. It seemed like he took the joy out of harassing the employees.

Naturally, I began to look for other jobs to remove myself from that situation. Even though it wasn't easy to get a new job, I still sent many applications without results. Finally, in my pursuit, I came across a post that said, "Please don't worry. I've got you – the universe." Since then, my life has started to turn around. I remembered *The Secret* and started reading the book, finishing it in a few days.

I learned about the law of attraction (law of attraction) in that book's pages. Since then, I've continued to learn more about law of attraction. As I continued to learn, I discovered that I had been using the law of attraction without realizing it. The negative thoughts and feelings I had led to me attracting more negativity. The feeling that I might lose my job wouldn't go away, and then with almost exact words, my boss fired me personally! I started to be more aware of my thoughts, feelings, and situations I put myself in to look for any negativity.

It became clear that law of attraction caused my negative thoughts to attract similar things, so it must do the same for the positive ones. So, I began my journey to build a purposeful life and conversed with the universe. Along the way, I learned that the universe is a mind reader; it lets you know exactly what you need. So, I've built a very intimate journey for guidance, to relieve stress, and to build a healthier mind/body connection between myself and the universe.

Most importantly, knowing that you won't start manifesting everything you want as soon as you begin practicing this law is essential. So, you'll want to change your mindset and practice patience. Remember that change doesn't happen overnight, but your wish can come true one day when you don't expect it.

Introduction to the law of attraction

Even if you don't realize it, the universe guides and influences your life in many ways. Still, the law of attraction is the strongest. This law impacts our lives in more ways than we can imagine. However, when you become aware of the law of attraction, you can use it to your advantage and change your life.

Every second we're all creating our realities because we will always be in a state of creation. Your thoughts, conscious and unconscious, create our future. Once you learn to use this powerful law in your life, you'll be able to guide your thoughts and actions to attract everything you want. Though many people have used the law of attraction to build their dream lives, others brush off the universal force as 'woo-woo.' So, if you're not convinced about the law of attraction, you aren't alone but as I've told people before: expect great things.

When you fully understand the law of attraction, your life and future will be what you make it. This guide will help you navigate your law of attraction journey with how the law works, how to do it, and one of the best techniques you can try.

What is the law of attraction?

As a universal principle this law states we attract what we focus on. So, whatever thoughts and actions you give attention to, the more they'll come into your life. When you think about the good aspects of your life, the more positive things will come your way; the same goes for the negatives in life.

You might have seen this law in action before. For instance, people who complain often attract others with negative attitudes. But conversely, this happens with happy people as they attract other positive people. Additionally, it's essential to know that the universe doesn't care what type of energy people put into the world; all it does is respond to your vibrations.

The good news is that you can change your vibrations to change how the universe reacts to you. You can manifest your desired outcomes by creating and leaning into a particular vibration. But, to do that, you'll need to be aware of thoughts, feelings, and energy and how they shape your reality. The law of attraction shapes the world in seven ways that can be described:

- **Law of Manifestation.** Many people think of this law when people talk about the law of attraction. It says that our feelings and thoughts shape our reality, and what we focus on will come into our life.

- **Law of Magnetism.** This law states that everything in your life, everything that's happened to you, and the things and opportunities you've come across come from the energy you radiate. So basically, you attract what you are.

- **Law of Unwavering Desire.** For this law to work, you need to want what you say you want. You need to be solid and unyielding to manifest your desires. A strong foundation is the only way you'll be able to attract what you want.

- **Law of Delicate Balance.** A balance in the universe makes up everything that exists; we even crave balance within ourselves. When we reach that balance, we find peace and happiness; to do this, we need to practice gratitude.

- **Law of Harmony.** When discussing this law, harmony means the flow of life, a coordinated interchange of forces and elements from the universe. Working in line with the universe's harmony makes things easier for us to get what the universe has to offer.

- **Law of Right Action.** Your words and actions impact your life as well as control the experiences you have. So, when you have positive interactions with the world, you will attract more of that.

- **Law of Universal Influence.** Even though the universe is infinitely more significant than we can comprehend, we're still an integral part of it. The things we think and do affect the world around us. That's why it's essential to be aware of our energy.

Many expert law of attraction advocates suggest that there are three primary axioms of the universal force:

Like Attracts Like

People use the law of attraction to manifest the life they want. This law seems simple, but it's more than just sitting and thinking that you want to be rich. There's more to manifesting your desires than that.

If you want to use the law of attraction to manifest your best life, it requires you to set your intentions when you describe what you want. Try to be open to new opportunities that come your way and be prepared to take any actions you might need to take. As well as sacrifice the things that don't serve you anymore.

This axiom, rightly named like attracts like, is something many have experienced at some point in their lives. For example, if you're having a bad day and things keep going wrong. Understandably, you'd be upset, but the more upset you became, the worse the day got. This is how the law of attraction works with negative energy.

Nature Abhors a Vacuum

The following principle is that nothing in the universe is empty. Every space gets filled with something, whether it's positive or negative. So, if you notice that you have many negative thoughts and influences you want to get rid of, you'll need to ensure that you fill that space with positivity.

For instance, if you work in a cluttered space, you might start feeling anxious, stressed, or have a feeling of claustrophobia. Then when you clean up your workspace, you have a sense of peace. The same concept works for our minds as well. So, getting rid of the negative thoughts and emotions that feed on negativity leaves room for creating positivity in our lives.

The Perfect Present

The last axiom is about showing gratitude and appreciating everything you currently have in your life. We must focus on the positivity and beauty of the moment. Unfortunately, there will always be thoughts, things, and occasions that make us unhappy, even if we've manifested all our desires and dreams. But showing gratitude will raise our vibrations to keep us in line with what we want.

It's essential to remember that you'll be starving the negatives in your life by being appreciative of everything, even the small stuff. But it'll also open doors of opportunity along the way.

Power of Manifestation

As humans, we all have hopes and dreams, but many don't know if they'll be able to reach them. So, how do you make your desires come true? The answer is practicing manifestation, which is feeling like you already achieved your goals and putting in the actions to make them accurate. You're essentially telling the universe that whatever you desire is yours. For manifestation to work for you, believing that what you want will be yours is essential. So, put yourself in the mindset that you've reached your dreams.

There are several ways you can use for manifestation. One way is through objects. Put all your positive energy and desires into an item of your choice. Some popular things people use are water and crystals. Later in this book, we will go over more manifestation techniques.

Power of Attraction

To get the law of attraction to work, you'll need to use these elements to remember the effectiveness of the power of attraction:

Know Your Desires.

Whatever you want in life is possible. Having said that, you need to be specific about what you want in life. Many people don't know exactly what they want but only have a general idea.

For example, people often say they want a brand-new house or a nice new car to earn more money; nevertheless, it isn't enough just to make a short statement. For manifestations to come true, you need to add more details. For example, you could say, 'I would love a new SUV, a gray Range Rover SE, with a Caraway interior. I can see myself driving down the highway on a nice summer day with my favorite song playing in the background. It's the greatest feeling.'

Being specific is the best way to ensure you get what you want. It's also helpful to add your feelings on what you're requesting. The vibrations of one's feelings undoubtedly make the law of attraction work.

It'll Come if You Believe.

Belief is the basis of manifesting; without belief, your manifestations won't come true; it's as simple as that. However, many people find it hard to believe in something they can't see, touch, or hear.

Well, the good news is that if you have doubts, you can start small. Ask for something small, something that there's no chance of you personally ever getting yourself.

That way, you'll know if your manifestation worked; it's not a coincidence since you wouldn't buy it yourself. So, think about what you're asking for and visualize it in your life. The more you think about this item, you'll start seeing more of it, and eventually, the universe will gift it to you. Once you feel confident in the law of attraction, you can begin to manifest bigger and better things.

Visualize Your Desires.

The ability to picture whatever you want in precise detail will do miracles to accomplish your manifestations. Visualization is one of the very best techniques to help manifest your specific desires. It's important to remember that if we desire something to take place in our lives, we must initially consider it.

For instance, say you want a car, envision owning your dream car, and picture yourself driving the vehicle in your everyday life. It's the same for everything you want to manifest. You first need to visualize it in your thoughts before it can come to you.

Inner Dialogue.

Consider this quote by Mahatma Gandhi that describes this concept, "Your beliefs become your thoughts, Your thoughts become your words, Your words become your actions, Your actions become your habits, Your habits become your values, Your values become your destiny." Everything you think of affects your actions and emotions.

So, infusing what you desire in life into your thoughts will change how you behave and your feelings. Also, when you invest what you want in life into your thinking, your unconscious mind automatically extends to work. It helps you find possibilities to make your desire real.

So, be aware of your internal discussion and change how you talk to yourself. Positive affirmations are a way to introduce new thoughts into your head. One positive thought lead to a hundred more positive thoughts.

Better Questions Trigger Better Answers.

To better understand this concept, think about the following questions. The first one is, why am I such a failure?

The second question is, exactly how can I improve to make myself more productive? Which question is better? It's the second one. When you ask questions, your unconscious mind will try to find solutions.

For example, if you ask the first question, your unconscious mind will find many answers to share why you certainly are a failure. Then, when you ask the second question, your unconscious mind will help you find precise solutions and develop creative techniques to be more successful.

The value of asking yourself the right questions is essential, so when you ask negative questions, turn them around, making them more positive and outcome focused.

Release Your Desire.

Once you've described a detailed account of what you want and believe it's on its way, the next step is to release your desire. Meaning never hold on too tight and keep hoping it shall come. Your passion is like a butterfly; if you hold on tight, you'll kill it. So instead, hold onto it lightly, and it can breathe and be free to enjoy life forever.

Gratitude.

Don't forget to appreciate anything you receive in life. When you do this, you're filling your thoughts and feelings with positive vibrating energy, which helps manifest more of your desires in life whenever you practice appreciation daily. Completing it with a good heart is crucial, not just doing it remotely.

Chapter 2: Explaining Vibrations

An aspect of the law of attraction is the law of vibrations which says we attract things that vibrate at the same frequency as our desires. Everything in the universe vibrates, including emotions, thoughts, objects, friends, and your dream job. Literally, everything has its own vibrational frequency. But what exactly are vibrations?

Your vibrational frequency is the rate the atoms in your body oscillate in your cells. All matter is made of atoms and makes up our reality. Everything in the universe is made of cells with a vibrational pattern that's either fast or slow. Something with a quick oscillation has a higher vibration or higher energy. At the same time, slow oscillating cells have a low vibration or low energy.

The law of vibration is essential for manifesting. Focusing on our vibrational frequency allows us to be efficient when creating change within ourselves and the world around us. If we change our cells' vibration, we change our reality.

It's important to note that your vibrations are connected to your intuition. For example, have you ever been around someone that makes you feel recharged and light? Or people that make you feel drained and heavy? This is your intuition picking up on other people's vibrations. In early human history, this was a survival instinct to keep us out of danger. Still, today not many people notice or listen to their intuition.

The law of vibration asks us to reconnect with the present. This ability to detect energized characteristics is closely related to our instinct and accounts for our sixth sense. But on the other hand, this law describes why we recognize traits about one another. So, we need to learn to trust this instinct and lean in.

Most of us choose to not listen to our intuition. However, your life can unravel differently if you lean into or ignore these intuitive pushes. So, take notice of what your body is telling you, and you'll be more familiar with precisely what is right for you. Typically, these nudges lead us closer to opportunities that make it easier to reach our desires.

Experiencing life separated from our instinct is like putting on a blindfold with headphones in and playing songs so loud that we can't hear anything else. But, on the other hand, the Universe bangs on our window to get our attention, so it can lead us to the door that will fulfill our needs. So, take the blindfold and headphones off, and listen.

Law of Vibration VS Law of Attraction

Since these two laws are similar, many people wonder what the difference between the two is. It's understandable why many people wonder about this. The answer is that they often work together.

The law of vibration happens before the law of attraction. You need to invoke the law of vibration by vibrating on the same frequency as your desires. Once you do this is when the law of attraction starts working in your favor.

More specifically, using the law of vibration means matching the vibrational frequency of your desires. While the law of attraction works alongside the law of vibration by providing you a way to create the frequency you want within yourself through several techniques such as meditation, visualization, and affirmations.

We must work with both laws whenever we want to manifest something. You draw your desires towards you when your thoughts align with the frequency of what you're trying to manifest.

When you utilize the law of vibration, you can attract your desires, work through difficult situations, and better understand your emotions and what you need to know about them.

Combining this law with the law of attraction makes manifesting the life you want easier. The vibrations you align with become your match, so you'll attract situations, experiences, and people that match your thoughts.

You can also use the law of vibrations to get through complex circumstances and situations.

For example, it might be tempting to blame external sources but look internally at thoughts and their vibrational frequency.

One of the best things about the law of vibration is how it helps you become more aware of your emotions and their purpose. Your emotions are a mirror of the level you're vibrating at. When you have positive emotions, it means you're at a higher frequency. When you have negative emotions, you're at a lower frequency. With this law, you can use your emotions to guide the direction of your thoughts and manifestations.

The Universe as a Vibrational Energy

The universe and everything in it are made of atoms that remain in a state of consistent movement. This suggests basically everything in the universe emits some form of energy as vibrations. All matter in the universe vibrates at a specific level, giving it its own frequency, created by the speed of its movement.

All microorganisms in this world use vibrational energy as the primary method of interaction. Vibrations are inaudible and unseen; however, when it comes to manifestation, the results become visible. Motion produces frequencies; consequently, this movement creates a sound even if we can't hear it. Each object's sound is identified by the frequency of the movement. So, that means things with different frequencies can affect us differently.

For example, your mindset can change depending on your music. For centuries, audio recovery has been utilized as a treatment to eliminate and treat numerous disorders. Multiple studies have revealed that the audio frequencies we pay attention to transform our brain's uniformity through our brain's auditory cortex. This impacts our feelings which triggers the release of hormones and chemicals with the capability to heal the body. Remarkably, ancient cultures realized this too:

- In Greek mythology, Apollo is the God of music and healing. Similarly, his son Aesculapius is said to heal mental disorders through songs.

- Some of the greatest philosophers, Plato and Aristotle, thought songs impacted the spirit and feelings.

It's also a common ancient practice for people to use adjusting forks to center and balance energies. However, our contemporary music's 12-tone range is somewhat out of sync with the old Solfeggio uniformities, a 6-tone range. A Benedictine monk named Guido d'Arezzo, c. 991 AD - c. 1050 AD, created this range 6-tone range which is mainly used in Gregorian Chants, which are thought to lead to spiritual blessings when sung consistently.

The Solfeggio range is slightly different today, with seven increasing notes marked by the notes commonly known as Do-Re-Mi-Fa-So-La-Ti. Initially, this sound range was marked by six ascending notes represented by Ut-Re-Mi-Fa-Sol-La, which came from an old hymn written about John the Baptist. Each note has its own benefits detailed below:

- Ut is 396 Hz: it transforms pain into delight, liberating shame & anxiety

- Re is 417 Hz: undoing negative situations and helping with adjusting to change

- Mi is 528 Hz: used for life improvement, bringing in miracles, and fixing DNA (utilized in over 100 Gregorian chants)

- Fa is 639 Hz: improve relationships and connect with spiritual family

- Sol is 741 Hz: for better expression, finding solutions, and addressing and cleansing

- La is 852 Hz: returning to an improved spiritual state

Many cultures use sound as a healing technique by using frequencies and sounds to repair problems within the body. It functions on the concept that all concerns are trembling at specific frequencies, including physical sickness, anxiety, depression, chronic disease, and stress.

Since these ailments have their own frequency, it alters and lower your energy level. Moreover, listening to different frequencies affects our brains, releasing hormones and chemicals to heal our bodies.

Each Solfeggio tone contains a frequency that helps regulate vibrations that keep you in good health in all aspects of your life including your body, mind, and spirit. The electromagnetic array encompasses numerous electromagnetic radiation wavelengths, such as x-rays, light, and radio waves. Also, it assists in envisioning the power of radiation figured out by the wavelength dimension.

Medical professionals and scientists agree that humans can only hear between 20 to 20,000 Hz. However, according to studies, humans can listen to audio frequencies outside this range, which will still influence us. For example, we can listen but not hear sounds as low as 12 Hz and as high as 28 kHz; though we can't hear these sounds, we can feel their vibrations.

Everything is Energy

Vibrations are a rhythm that occurs in a wide range, like changing seasons and tidal patterns. In addition, they happen inside you. We can see this in our heartbeats, breathing, and circadian rhythms.

There are likewise smaller vibrational rhythms inside your body. For instance, particles in each of your cells shake at set intervals. On top of that, researchers have discovered resonances on the nano level using atomic force microscopes- much smaller than a strand of human hair. In addition, researchers have found that vibrations trigger cell modifications, which may affect your system's features. Heat, for example, can change the rate of the molecule's vibrations.

The Energy of All Things

Researchers have understood that consistent thoughts and habits affect the rhythms within you. For instance, distressed thinking activates the launch of anxiety hormonal agents that cause your heart rate to speed up or slow down. Similarly, music's audio frequencies influence thoughts, feelings, and the human body systems.

Professionals studying vibrational energy accept that our activities and thoughts can alter more minor rhythms in our bodies. Advocates believe it's possible to boost or decrease our vibrations by changing our habits, ideas, and surroundings. Altering those nano vibrations might ripple to our external lives, affecting our physical and mental states.

The expanding research studies suggest a vital link between your mind and body. Advocates assume you may modify your body's vibrations to:

- alter your state of mind
- improve your physical health
- help you attain your intentions and goals

Additionally, it's widely accepted that certain emotions and routines, such as peace, approval, and happiness, produce high-frequency vibrations. In contrast, sensations, and states of mind such as rage, misery, and fear have lower vibrations.

Positive and Negative Vibrations

It's common for people to talk about someone's vibe in a particular circumstance or environment. The energy they give off gets specified as either positive or negative vibrations. The individual's vibrations result from several variables, including mindset, experience, assumed patterns, and assumptions of the world.

Every person has a one-of-a-kind inner map of their external truths based on exactly how they have reacted to life experiences. This, subsequently, develops our belief systems and identity.

Positive vibrations are high frequency, assuming practices, emotions, and perspectives. In contrast, negative vibrations are low-frequency reasoning patterns, mindsets, and thoughts.

So, if you've been in a constant state of negative thinking, change the tone of your interior dialogue. Offer consideration to what you are telling yourself. Your mind and body will certainly respond to the resonance of your idea patterns. Switching the tone to be more optimistic will create an instant shift in your vibrations.

How Vibrations Work

You'll only attract the energy that matches the energy you're putting out; the same goes for vibrations. So, this universal law aids you in establishing how you really feel in a situation or scenario at any minute. Thoughts additionally hold vibrational frequencies and working with this law can help you understand them.

Based upon this doctrine, every little thing is made from energy, and we can match the energy of anything we seek to materialize. Therefore, this rule can assist us in evaluating our current situation and creating a bountiful life incorporated with the other universal laws.

Manifesting. To manifest anything, we must initially match the resonance of what it is we're looking for. You'll only attract things that match your energy. Remember that your thoughts also have vibrations.

For example, the view "I need even more money" holds a vibration of absence and might lead to a self-fulfilling revelation.

Navigating Situations. This law can help you identify how you feel in a scenario or circumstance at any given time. Once you recognize high vibrational attitudes, areas, and individuals that feel healthy, and interesting—it gets easier to sense when you are in higher vibrations.

Managing Emotions. Emotions hold vibrational frequencies and collaborating with this law can assist you in navigating them. Feelings are powerful guides to shift us into a more significant, balanced state of being. Emotions can range from low frequency (fear, shame, and so on) to high frequency (delight and love).

However, there are no bad feelings-all energy wants to move forward. The law of vibration assists us in recognizing when we're loaded with dense, heavy feelings, so we can let them go and preserve a greater frequency.

When Will You Notice a Change?

You'll start seeing results from law of attraction after about a month. Afterward, it should be a lot easier to manifest your wishes. Your doubts, as well as worry, will go away.

Also, you ought to feel more hopeful concerning your intentions. Keep in mind that you attract what you envision. It'll ultimately show up when you think and act as if you've already achieved your desires.

Raising Your Vibrations

It's common today to hear people talk about another person's vibe; we subconsciously can pick them up as humans. For instance, have you ever met a person who attracts you to them or someone who makes you want to avoid them? It's not just people who give off vibes but situations as well.

For example, if you see a shocking story on the news, you start feeling heavy. Yet, on the other hand, if you see a puppy carry a stick that's bigger than it, you really feel a warmth inside.

As mentioned earlier in this book, whatever energy you put out is what will come back to you, which is the basis of law of attraction. This law states that you shape your reality through manifestation according to your thoughts and feelings.

Every little thing in deep space is composed of atoms oscillating at different rates, nature, situations, feelings, animals, inanimate objects, literally everything. At the same time, even humans have their own vibrations, from your fingernails to the flow of your thoughts.

In standard terms, everything has a vibration level, whether lower with slow or high with fast movements. Likewise, everything has a natural energy level that we pick up on. This is our instinct; with it, you can feel someone's energy when you're around them.

You feel lighter, happier, and more secure when you vibrate at a higher level. In contrast, lower vibrations make you feel sad, heavy, and confused. Most spiritual practices around the world point towards this higher realm of awareness. Also, clinical research studies, like those by Dr. David Hawkins, have even determined that different frequency levels create a range of understanding.

Now that you know what vibrations are, just exactly how are you vibrating? Below are twelve ways you can increase your vibrations.

1. Showing Gratitude

Appreciation for what you have is the fastest and easiest way to increase your vibrations. However, it's something that we must work towards. As Larissa Gomez stated, "Being thankful is not always experienced as a natural state of existence. We must work at it, akin to a type of strength training for the heart."

When you feel yourself experiencing low energy feelings, see if you can alter your attention to thankfulness by focusing on the good things in your life.

It can be something big or small, such as having your favorite snack, the sun shining, or having people you love in your life. Make gratitude a routine; it will undoubtedly transform your view of life as you start to experience spiritual awareness as well as gratitude for the little things.

2. Show and Experience Love

Get in touch with someone you love and hold that person in your heart. Envision the two of you sitting across from you and pay attention to how you feel at that moment. Do you have a feeling of lightness, growth, and joy? These feelings will consume you, which is the change you seek. Showing and experiencing love is another high vibrational state you can be in. It also has the power to draw you out of your darkest moments. Open your heart to love, and your vibrations will soar.

3. Be Kind to Yourself

Anytime you're unwilling to give something you have a lot of, such as love, passion, or money, it lowers your vibrations and adds negativity to your life. At the same time, if you put your happiness into something outside yourself, it'll leave you making you feel inadequate.

So, it's essential that you are kind to yourself and find your own happiness. You can also be kind to others to raise your vibrations.

4. Focus on Breathing and Meditation

When you work on existing in the moment, your vibrations resonate harmoniously with reality's higher vibrational aspects. Remember that the only reality is the present; the past and future only exist in your mind.

Focusing on breathing and meditation likewise calms your nervous system, enhances your state of mind, and creates even more substantial feelings of peace. This spiritual technique helps increase your energy level promptly to ensure you can delight in the advantage of high vibrational qualities; without delay to benefit your well-being.

5. Forgive Yourself and Others

Abraham-Hicks, a well-known spiritualist, came up with a scale for emotional guidance that ranks emotions by their vibrational level. Emotions range from 1 being the highest vibration to 22 being the lowest. On this list, blame is number 15, and guilt is number 21, so if you hold on to these feelings, you're lowering your vibrations.

Moreover, suppose you practice forgiveness and mercy. In that case, you'll let go of these low energies that are weighing you down and start moving towards higher emotions at the top of the scale. Additionally, it's important to be forgiving and merciful to others as well as yourself.

6. Have a Diet with High Vibration Foods

You will undoubtedly lower your vibration if you eat a lot of low-energy things like processed and fried foods.

Instead, when you eat high vibrational foods like unprocessed foods, fruits, and vegetables, it'll show an increase in your energy level. These high vibration foods increase your vibrational frequency.

7. Limit your Consumption of Alcohol and Other Toxins

While it can briefly feel exceptional, alcohol is a downer as well as a low vibrational substance. To have a clear, healthy, and balanced overview of life, you'll need to limit toxins in your body as a starting point.

Later, you can work on eliminating the use of these substances altogether. As opposed to trying to numb out the world around you, accept a lot more healthful and all-natural lifestyle choices and see if you do not feel much more plentiful.

8. Be Aware of your Thoughts

What your thoughts focus on will come to be, and these thoughts will shape your future. So, suppose your thoughts are pessimistic, negative, or overly worried.

In that case, you will likely be put in more situations that foster these feelings. Equally, as appreciation attracts more of the same into your life, so do rashness, unworthiness, and envy. This unfavorable outcome can lead to you feeling strained, heavy, and overwhelmed.

So, be diligent about what you focus your thoughts on. Press away negative energy and select positive thoughts, for they are the method to positive change.

9. View Entertainment with High Vibrations

Your life force is not restricted to the food you eat; it consists of every little thing you take, including entertainment. Make sure whatever you view for entertainment is of high vibration as well as makes you feel energized instead of drained. To figure this out, you can ask yourself some questions; for example, does being on social media make you feel stimulated or exhausted?

Does that violent action movie increase your state of mind, or does it add to your anxiety? How does the music you listen to every day make you feel afterward? Just precisely how might you alter the soundtrack of your everyday commute to something that changes your state of mind and adds to the rest of your day? It's essential to be careful concerning your media consumption as you have to do with the food you eat. Doing this will increase your vibrations as you move throughout your day.

10. Your Environment

At the same time, your environment around you can also affect vibrations, how you feel, and your life. So, ensure that your home and work atmospheres forever show positive emotions such as interest, excitement, passion, and appeal.

You can try adding art, plants, colors, special lights, and painting the walls, to improve the feel of your space. In addition, lowering any mess or clutter creates space for quality, clearness, and productivity.

11. Spend Time Outside

This tip has two benefits for boosting your vibration: going outdoors and exercising outside. Take a break from constantly being around electricity and get some sun on your face.

If you spend a couple of mindful minutes outside, you can change your state of mind. Choosing to go for a walk around your neighborhood when you're feeling low energy can be helpful in raising your vibrations.

12. Build High Vibration Relationships

Surround yourself and build relationships with individuals that make you feel energized instead of drained. Invest your time with individuals who make you feel better about being yourself and being on your own.

People who believe in you and want to reverberate at a high frequency just like you. Funneling positive energy into elevating your friends and family consistently is one of the best things you can do for the world and yourself. This is the only method you can add to increasing the cumulative awareness of the world.

Foundation of Energy – Uncovering the Essence of Mind and Body

All things in our world are regularly moving and shaking. Also, something that appears fixed still oscillates at different regularities. Resonance is a sort of motion specified by oscillation between 2 states. As well undoubtedly, all issues resonate with numerous underlying fields.

The radical reaction is that it's everything about vibrations. However, over the past years, scientists have developed a "resonance theory of consciousness" that suggests that regularity is the basis of human awareness and the real world. These questions are all components of the old "mind-body issue," which has stood to a generally gratifying last idea for many years.

A fantastic sensation occurs when numerous shaking things/processes become part of closeness: they commonly begin to tremble with each other simultaneously after a little bit. They "sync up," sometimes in a manner that can appear weird. This is discussed today as the feeling of spontaneous self-organization. Analyzing this sensation leads to possibly deep insights concerning the nature of consciousness and the universe.

We agree that vibrational energies are the critical device behind human consciousness. Moreover, as I'll talk about below, they are the standard system for all physical communications.

Stephen Strogatz supplies different circumstances from physics, chemistry, biology, as well as neuroscience to illustrate what he calls "sync" (synchrony) in his 2003 publication, also called sync, consisting of:

- Vibration is a universal sensation at the heart of what can usually look like mystical tendencies toward self-organization.

- Significant neuron firing can occur in human minds at information regularities. Animal understanding is believed to be generally connected to different kinds of neuronal synchrony.

- The moon's switching is exactly synced with its orbit around the Planet such that we continuously see the same face.

- These names explain the rate of electrical oscillations in the countless mind locations, as identified by electrodes placed beyond the head.

  Gamma waves are commonly specified as 30 to 90 hertz, theta as 4 to 7 Hz, and beta as 12.5 to 30 Hz. These aren't challenging cutoffs; their standards vary in different ranges.

- Lasers are created when photons of the exact same power, as well as uniformity, are produced together.

Pascal Fries, a German neurophysiologist, has discovered just how electric patterns work together in the brain to develop human awareness.

Synchronization, in terms of regular electrical oscillation rates, permits smooth interaction between nerve cells and teams of nerve cells. Without comprehensibility (synchronization), inputs turn up at random phases of the nerve cell excitability cycle. As a result, they are ineffective, or a minimum, a lot less effective, in interaction.

Over the past years, researchers have created a "resonance concept of awareness" that suggests that resonance is the basis of human awareness and our physical reality. It's every little thing concerning vibrations, yet it's likewise relating to the kind of resonances and, most significantly, concerning shared resonances.

Over the previous years, researchers have established a "resonance theory of awareness" that suggests that regularity is the basis of human consciousness and the physical globe. As a result, the mind-body issue was rebranded over the last 2 years and is commonly known as the "hard problem" of awareness.

These names explain the speed of electric oscillations in the numerous mind areas, as established by electrodes placed beyond the head. Pascal Fries, a German neurophysiologist, has checked out how electric patterns function together in the brain to produce human recognition. Examining this phenomenon results in a possibly deep understanding worrying the nature of consciousness and the cosmos.

The resonance theory of consciousness builds upon the job of Pascal fries and numerous others to generally assist in discussing human understanding and recognition.

Chapter 3: Law of attraction in Physics

Quantum physics is the innovative science of our time. It describes clinically what a great deal of the outstanding researchers like Einstein mentioned and proposed but can't show.

Doing "absolutely nothing" and getting something is not what most people think. It's a scientific reality that your ideas develop your reality.

For example, one of the straightest connections between quantum physics and the law of attraction originates from The Onlooker Impact. This proves that particles develop when we put our power into observing them.

Quantum physics, as well as the law of attraction, works together. However, many individuals are skeptical regarding this law of attraction business. It sounds very "ventilated fairy" and like an empty promise.

Quantum physics can help us explain how the law of attraction works. But more significantly, it describes that the law of attraction is factual. This is exciting news, especially with the backing of quantum physics, since it suggests that there is no restriction to what you can materialize when you understand the law of attraction.

What Is Quantum Physics?

Let's start with a summary of what quantum physics is. First, everything in the universe is composed of atoms. Your vibrations as a human being aren't fixed, as with many natural items. However, you have the power to determine what resonance you remain in by deliberately choosing your thoughts.

If you examine your life, you will undoubtedly recognize that it represents your most common thoughts.

Any individual, not just quantum physicists performing experiments, can observe the law of attraction. We have all seasoned strictly how negative thoughts just seem to attract a lot more, and often even worse, negative thoughts. The law of vibration has an extra clinical connection to quantum physics and, more precisely, defines the sensations of showing up.

Power particles act under the awareness of the onlooker. All fragments are made up of smaller-sized bits called subatomic particles or quanta. Perhaps you desired a particular car and truck and began seeing the same version everywhere you went.

One significant takeaway from these clinical concepts around the regulation of attraction is that with the Viewer Result, you can bring suggestions into existence. Additionally, you understand the where, what, and how power materializes based on the onlooker's mind.

Maybe you have had the remarkable experience of everything integrating, with one thing going right after the next in unforeseen ways. This resonance or motion of bits is what we call energy. This power is made up of your thoughts, emotions, and beliefs. The value that was determined differed concerning the onlooker. You are the onlooker to your own life. This attraction process has been studied medically using quantum physics and quantum mechanics.

The Big Bang theory describes that whatever is in deep space took off right into being from the exact same source. This implies that whatever is in deep space is knotted or connected with every little thing. Simply specified, like attracts like.

The guidelines of physics are the same even when the particles are as small as quanta. However, most recognize Newtonian physics, which applies to everyday items we can see with the naked eye. The patterns videotaped on the screen are diffraction and interference, showing that particles operate as both waves and issues.

Quantum physics is not so simple. To start with, when an observer views fragments, they really act in different ways than when they are not being watched. This quantum phenomenon is called The Onlooker Effect. These particles remain in a continuous state of movement. Also, 'dead items' like rock are bits relocating at a high resonance that can't be viewed with the naked eye.

The Principles of Quantum Entanglement

Quantum entanglement is the phenomenon that occurs when 2 bodies are connected to one another or intertwined. The entangled objects work as one, regardless of their distance. Having a much deeper understanding will certainly assist and prepare the information in your mind and allow you to use it better. As well as the one thing every individual has complete control over affecting is their thoughts. When we think about something, we are interacting with that point.

Knowing something will cause its existence in your reality. Researchers determined that waves of power fragments have potential, not specific, movements and places in space. This final thought transpired since observation caused the information to assume just one arbitrary feasible value out of the whole collection of possibilities.

This implies that all fragments of power have an unlimited field of possibilities bordering them. Also, the onlooker is the one who chooses just how that energy will materialize.

While the law of attraction is most extensively understood and comprehended, the critical regulation is the regulation of resonance. This enables you and gives you the power to determine what you draw into your life.

When energies with the same vibrations straighten, they are drawn into one another. The indication is not a theory; it is a reality. As a matter of fact, you've been

using this principle all your life to materialize
whatever you want.

Merely, what you think shapes the truth you perceive.
Likewise, the power you produce through your ideas
identifies the items, people, and scenarios that will
undoubtedly turn up in your life. It is common to
listen to the term "showing up" today.

The word is typically utilized to explain intentionally
bringing things right into your life (be they good or
bad points) via your energy. By offering it sufficient
energy, it somewhat enters your life and materializes
in physical form.

Law of attraction in Quantum Physics

You now recognize that all bits of power in deep space
are knotted. All power bits are bordered by a field of
unlimited capacity for habits, area, and form. Similar
to terms, your observation of bits creates them and
brings them to life.

Observing, offering, and concentrating power on what
is not yet present in your life immediately makes it
real via the principle of The Observer Effect. The
"Double Slit Experiment" developed this policy, where
a beam of electrons is fired at an aircraft with two
slits. After going through the slits, the electrons strike
a screen.

Answer is Intention

Manifesting involves more than determination and
conviction. While every person attracts their desires
differently, numerous rely on the same standard
techniques. Yet, first, you need to be particular about
what you desire.

A substantial variable is crucial for whatever you desire: make your intentions as specific as possible. The even more concise and clear, the better.

For example, instead of simply saying, you want to find your soulmate, build a comprehensive picture of what he or she looks like; think about their top qualities, attributes, values, and so forth.

Some experts think the best times to manifest are at the beginning of the month, the start of the week, or in the early morning. But any time is great to start fresh with a positive intention.

Recognize Desire

To set intents, you need to identify your needs first. It may be big or small, something, like investing in a new vehicle or house. Attempt to keep your purpose linked to being a place of abundance versus a place of lack.

The wish might be to develop an area of abundance. Still, the feeling you have underneath it is necessary to accomplish your objective. You can put language to it and compose the purpose as soon as you recognize the surface.

Get Clear on Yourself

Objectives are about doing, and intentions are about being. The doing becomes more easily accessible when you pay attention to what you require to achieve your objectives. You can do this by journaling on the high qualities you want to embody that will sustain you in achieving your purpose.

Decide Particular Action Steps

Purposes are not one-size-fits-all. Objectives, such as "being healthier," can suggest items that are incredibly varied to different people. Therefore, getting details about the actions you'll take to satisfy your intent and complying with them is vital.

Being specific will result in success in achieving your goals. As a result, as soon as you have the intention to be healthier, focus on your goals by establishing smaller waypoints like: "I'll work out 3 times this week."

Shift Any Limiting Beliefs

Not thinking about your intent is a usual challenge that can impede manifestations. Try changing your state of mind to align your ideas and needs if you're experiencing this.

If you don't believe it's possible, search for where love is contained in your life if you plan to find love in someone.

Surrender and Lean into Faith

When we establish an option, we use it as a lorry to control our lives. But, still, there is a function of confidence and abandonment- a peaceful receptiveness. So, if you're struggling with managing your intents, take a step back and forget any resistance you locate.

Objectives are not established as a rock; they're targets that can move, change, and progress as we expand. So, essentially, there's no feeling in emphasizing over establishing objectives. Instead, give yourself consent to alter and adjust your dreams as you obtain them, which in turn aids you in releasing control over the scenario.

Pygmalion and Golem Effect

The Pygmalion and Golem effects results are both based on the idea of self-fulfilling revelations. For instance, consider a study where an instructor is told what level each of their pupils is at academically before starting their brand-new course at the beginning of the academic year.

The researchers of this experiment administered a pre-test to a group of primary trainees. After that, they told the educators names of students they believed were late bloomers. They stated that these pupils were expected to be less successful academically this year.

The researchers had drawn names arbitrarily from a hat to determine the student names to provide the teachers. These students weren't ranked on their performance on the pre-test. They were all chosen arbitrarily. The instructor understands which team of students has a high degree and recognizes the other group with an ordinary academic degree.

At the end of the year, which group was more academically successful? Well, the group of students declared as academically talented executed the most effectively. But, on the other hand, the "ordinary" group performed lower than anticipated. And the unknown pupils were someplace in between the ordinary students as well as the gifted students.

Eight months later, the researchers examined the whole group of students. Furthermore, they discovered that the students they told the instructors would grow academically were significantly more successful than the remainder of the trainees.

The pupils were picked randomly, so how did they score more than everyone else? Does this mean the instructor was told the smartest were the most academically talented?

No, because they believed they would undoubtedly be more successful academically, the instructors dealt with those students differently during the remainder of their course.

Educators were even more supportive of pupils that they thought would become smarter. However, they didn't apply many initiatives to students that weren't expected to do well academically.

Generally, your energy and assumptions are shown to those around you. Therefore, you will undoubtedly draw in unfavorable results if you're an adverse person. But, on the other hand, you will certainly bring positive results if you have an excellent can-do perspective.

Consequently, the youngsters started to think of themselves differently and did much better because of this effect. Moreover, the students were transformed by their teachers' reasonable expectations. This is referred to as the Pygmalion effect. The opposite holds true of the Golem effect. The negative reinforcement of teachers' lower assumptions made students think they were substandard to others.

How It Functions

It doesn't mean that your unconscious mind will undoubtedly follow because you believe something at a conscious level. All your integrated routines make up how you react to day-to-day scenarios.

Spontaneous acts, features, and patterns are deeply hidden in your subconscious. You've been programmed to act the way you do from your youth. As a kid, every little thing that you observed with your conscious mind poured into your subconscious.

You need to change your paradigm as the standard adjustments, your vibration will change. As a result, your life will certainly alter. If you activate your consciousness, bring awareness to your ideas, and change your state of mind over time, your standard will undoubtedly change. You'll produce new behaviors. Your outcomes will vary.

By repetitively claiming a brand-new method of reasoning, your paradigm will change. And your activities are regulated by your paradigm. You'll bring in points that agree with your new vibration. You'll bring in people that are in harmony with your brand-new beat.

If you don't like your scenario or the fact of your life, your paradigm is the issue.

Well, the group of trainees proclaimed academically gifted executed the best. And the unknown trainees were someplace between the typical students and the talented pupils. Suppose the paradigm was developed by the repetition of behaviors. In that case, you'll need to repeatedly be uncomfortable if you desire your life to transform.

Allow first to divide your brain into two components: the subconscious mind and the conscious mind. The subconscious mind regulates parts of your body that frequently require to be controlled without always attracting your interest to these responsibilities. An example of this would be your breath.

They then told the educators names of pupils they thought were late bloomers. Rosenthal and Jacobsen had drawn names arbitrarily from a hat to decide the student names to offer the teachers. The students were changed by their instructors' favorable assumptions.

You don't have to react to situations. You can begin continually executing affirmations into your life and repeating them on your own. But, of course, I'm not stating that simply claiming a phrase will alter your life.

Chapter 4: How Thoughts and Words Can Lead to Your Journey

Words and thoughts can affect your vibrations positively or negatively; they control what comes into your life. For example, you can make somebody ill, feel bad about themself, make them cry, or feel satisfied and happy with the power of your words.

Many of us have been in situations where numerous coworkers spoke negatively to an individual they work with. For example, they may make fun of them for their looks, the way they dress, or any other thing. Let's call this employee Bob. After several hours of hearing his coworkers' comments, he feels unwell. Of course, there was nothing physically wrong with Bob; it was the power of spoken words from the people he relied on.

Before the words leave your mouth, the thought must be in your head. So, when you hear people's words, you get an idea of how people think. Everything we say either influences another person or ourselves. You can utilize this power positively or negatively.

Dr. Emoto's famous experiment on water confirmed that words have vibrations and will undoubtedly modify the framework of water crystals. He proved that you can, in fact, change the molecular structure of water with the power of words.

In this experiment, Dr. Emoto had several vials of water and labeled some of the vials with negative words. On other vials, he put positive words on them. The comments on the labels were also spoken and repeated aloud. He then examined the icy water crystals under a microscope. The ones with positive words were beautiful, while the ones with unfavorable damaging comments were hideous, warped water crystals.

So below is something to consider. The body is 60% water, our lungs are 83% water, and the mind and heart are 73% water. Since we are mainly water, it makes you think about what our words are doing to us. It's essential to consider how our words alter the water in our bodies or others.

If you continue to think about this, things will begin to change for you. You would undoubtedly attract what you want in your life. So, work on transforming your thoughts and words to produce a better future.

Words You Speak and Think

Our words program our world, lives, and reality. The words we speak and think about are powerful devices we can utilize to develop our reality. In that case, it's essential that we choose our words wisely to create our ideal life.

The things we think have an effect on what turns up in the lives we live. Yet the power we have hinges on our words and thoughts. They furnish strong affirmations to shape our innermost ideas. They validate exactly how we see others, our lives, and ourselves. So why do we abuse our most effective property?

In our current society, we're accustomed to talking about the problems and negative feelings we have. When we constantly talk about and focus on negative experiences, people, and thoughts we bring more of that into our world. That means when we actively compliment or grumble about what's happening in our lives, we're allowing negativity to manifest in our reality. When you focus your energy on something, your words and thoughts manifest no longer simply in your mind, and others will begin to think of you in that way as well.

Ask yourself, do you want to tell people that you are unsuccessful, unlucky, miserable, or any other negative thoughts you have about yourself? Especially, since you understand that these specific words are establishing the lifestyle you want to live. Remember it's a journey so start by trying to choose the words you use deliberately. Doing this boosts your self-awareness of how your words impact your reality.

You develop your own world, and the things you say go. Subsequently, when you are about to use unfavorable words, try picking ones that will have a more positive effect on your life. For instance, on a day you aren't feeling your best you might say 'I am so unhealthy,' try instead to attempt to transform this into a more positive declaration. You can try saying, 'I am working on being healthier, and I am getting closer to reaching my goal every day.'

You are your wishes, hopes, and successes, this shows when you use two of the most effective words, a person can say; 'I am.' Even though these two words are small they are extremely reliable and are among the most beneficial words in your vocabulary. Subsequently, how we use 'I am' in a sentence informs us who we are, not only to ourselves but to everyone else as well.

When you say things like, 'I am lazy' or 'I am successful,' that's the reality you'll produce for yourself. So, select your words carefully, and ensure that what you say comes from a positive place. It's essential you do this when you talk about yourself, the life you want, and other people. Your thoughts and words become your reality, so choose and use them wisely.

Words You Speak to Others

Words and the law of attraction are essential in speaking with others. Therefore, to truly benefit from this spiritual practice, you should commit to becoming a blessing to others through your words and activities.

Everyone has been wounded by words. However, a few of us have gaping openings in our hearts from the harmful things said about us. Keep this in the front of your mind: Nobody knows the pain another person has gone through. Therefore, there is no demand for shredding anybody's spirit with harsh words or ridicule.

Your only purpose here on Earth is to positively impact everyone who connects with you. And, yes, I recognize that some people will be challenging. But remember that the universe allowed them on your path for a reason.

Maybe the second most challenging point you will certainly need to make is to find a way to not lash out when someone talks negatively about you. This includes talking about them behind their back. When you gossip, you don't just make yourself look classless; you remove yourself from the creative flow of the Universe.

There is a lot of research, both in publications and online, about talking compassionately to one another. So, I have tried to distill my emphasis down to a few suggestions.

- Ensure that your words are kind
- Listen carefully to what others are saying
- Be considerate of others' experiences
- Validate people's feelings
- Try not to tell them how to handle their situation
- Talk gently, humbly, and from your heart
- Letting others know that you understand can be recovering to a damaged heart
- Never use their own words to put them down when they are vulnerable with you

Transforming yourself to ensure that you are open to the wonders ever-present in the law of attraction begins with self-awareness of how you speak.

Then, every circumstance is a possibility to extend healing words so that conversations and connections come to be positive and corrective. The words you use and the law of attraction work together in shaping reality.

Words You Speak to the Universe

Chatting with the Universe is a petition, and the petition is one of the most influential forces we can use to converse with forces beyond us.

This form of communication changes who you are and the situations surrounding you. The Universe wants to fill your life with abundance as well as be blessed and unafraid. This communication takes two forms when using the law of attraction:

- First, you need to firmly ask what you want and declare that the Universe's blessings will happen in your life.

- Secondly, you must appreciate the blessings the Universe has already given you and the ones it'll provide you in the future.

To live a life of abundance, you need to use restorative words of faith to use the Universe's power to change your reality. Constantly working on your relationship with the Universe is life changing.

 Truthfully, being mindful of my words and thoughts has helped me build the life I want. Talk about what you are looking for; your comments and the law of attraction are delicately attached throughout the Universe.

Your Words Create Your Reality

Like many others, I've been in situations where I constantly talked about how miserable I was at my job. I would say things like, "But it's been difficult for me to find a new job," or "There's simply nothing out there."

At the time, I didn't know that my negative thoughts were shaping my reality and keeping me from finding a job. When I learned about the law of attraction, I learned to remain optimistic. It cemented in my mind exactly how easily words can develop a self-fulfilling prophecy.

The words you speak hold power to create brand-new opportunities or close doors for you. It has the power to build strong relationships or damage them. Power to raise people or to draw them down, yourself included.

We commonly don't understand how impactful our words are on ourselves and others. If we did, we would certainly do far, much less grumbling! You would use negative expressions less that threaten your power and limit your future somehow, albeit unintentionally.

The words you speak develop the reality you inhabit. Your mind, body, and environment will follow whatever instructions your comments lead.

For example, use positive words about yourself, your skills, your goals, and your troubles; you'll start seeing more positivity. Similarly, you'll attract more negativity if you consistently claim things that verify incompetence, resemble despondence, support stress, or fuel pessimism.

It might seem extravagant, but your world will morph to mirror your words in time. It's, therefore, essential to be deliberate about the words you use and talk in ways that empower and broaden rather than decrease value.

Transforming traditional methods of thinking and speaking isn't something you can do overnight. Nonetheless, neuroscientists have discovered that with repeated practice, you can reshape your brain and change negative thought patterns and habits with positive ones.

So, when you blunder, don't batter on yourself or label yourself a 'lost cause.' That's precisely the kind of thinking you have to stop using. Instead, accept your fallibility, and refocus on what you want.

Three Steps to law of attraction

There are three steps to use the law of attraction to your advantage. First, you can utilize this procedure to make any changes you want in your life.

For example, you can find the perfect partner, get a great body, enhance your wellness, age gracefully, and help inspire goodness worldwide.

Step 1: Identify Your Desires

Most individuals are familiar with the expression "Ask, Believe, Receive." While "Ask" is considered the primary step of production of the law of attraction. Asking is a vital part of this universal law. So, before you ask, be sure it is what you truly desire. To start, go somewhere quiet where you can be alone and sit and review life. Then, get your computer, journal, or notepad and let the creative ideas stream. Ask yourself questions to discover your wants, for example:

- What do I want in life?
- How will I accomplish my desires?
- What do I need?
- What am I passionate about?
- What things make me happy?

Dream big and be creative when figuring out your desires, much like a kid. Youngsters believe they can do anything as well as do it well. We often tend to shed that thought as we age and make mistakes. However, mistakes are a part of life, enabling us to adjust, change and grow. We can indeed have, be, and do anything we want.

As you do this, compose whatever comes to your mind. Allow only good thoughts and sensations to move through you. Good feelings are the trick to identifying your desires during this process. If your desires scare you just a little bit, that's fine. Actually, that's great! It indicates that your vision and potential are big enough to attain it. So, keep visualizing them.

Step 2: Believe You'll Accomplish Your Goals

The following step is believing you'll get what you want. At this phase, you deliberately visualize how you want your life to look. Later, you enable yourself to feel that belief being satisfied. You need to have unshakable faith that you'll get precisely what you want in life. As you envision this, you strongly understand that it is currently on its way!

Things don't always happen quickly, but that's all right; staying optimistic is essential. Unfortunately, rashness or questioning can sneak in during this phase and reverse the development. Give yourself time every day to feel hope, belief, strength, and enthusiasm. You should also release questions, concerns, and fear during this time.

Keep your actions aligned with your intentions and desires. Unfavorable emotions don't serve you. It is an illusion to hold you back. Stay in the moment and allow time to simply exist in the moment. There are also three emotions you need to get through the belief:

- **Toughness:** To have firm intentions, you need to have inner strength. Having desires come from a place of want, so it's crucial to maintain positive ideas, words, and actions. Your good intention will ultimately attract your desires.

  You know your wishes are in your best interest; however, you will be tempted to fall back into old routines that keep you from what you want to attract. Positive energy wants you; however, so does the negative they both want to expand.

  Throughout the spiritual world, we are told not to succumb to temptation because blessings can be taken from you as quickly as they are given.

- **Trust:** Your belief system's efficiency is built on trust. What you feel can only hold true for you if you believe your thoughts will ultimately attract what you want to your life. If you think your ideas won't attract your best life, they won't. Remember that the law of attraction functions both ways; it can bring you what you want and get you what you don't want. So, it depends on you to trust the process to work for you.

- **Gratefulness:** Being grateful is the most vital aspect of universal law. However, the Universe doesn't give you everything you want in one fell swoop.

  Instead, it gives you little bits of the puzzle to create your dream life. You must trust that each little piece is supplied for your best interest and appreciate it. Being thankful for your desires like you already have them is the cornerstone of the recipe for success.

Depending on your thoughts and expectations, this part of the process can take the longest. The amount of time it takes relies on you. Stay focused, determined, and patient that it will undoubtedly happen while remaining open to it. Prospective mistakes and obstacles can occur, and that's alright; that's part of the journey. However, you constantly find out something new and grow more.

Step 3: Succeed and Receive

When the law of attraction starts working, praise yourself and celebrate! You deserve it! Your excitement will help the manifestation process come to fruition and can even accelerate and surpass your expectation. Be mindful of your feelings and assess the true power that you've always had within you. You can accomplish success in anything you apply these principles to.

Bear in mind this isn't something you have just activated because you understand it; it's been working the whole time. Currently, you know exactly how to harness your power via the law of attraction. Every idea, word, and action develop a co-creation with you and the Universe. Therefore, you do have the limitless power of co-creation.

Consciously using the law of attraction to your advantage can bring success beyond what you thought was possible. The potential for everything lies in the Universe; however, the capability to harness it exists in you.

Manifestation Techniques

Manifestation suggests producing or transforming something from a concept into reality. That indicates that any technique or strategy used to bring a desire or goal to life could be considered a manifestation technique.

 In practice, though, when many people consider manifesting, they think of the mental procedures, for example, ideas, feelings, and beliefs, that assist us in producing the truth we desire.

The good news is that clinical research studies have shown many reliable ways to manifest what we want. Unfortunately, the bad news is that pseudo-scientific studies have spread throughout the Web. As a result, many manifestation approaches likely don't help many people. So, let's begin by clarifying which techniques are science-based.

Power of Action

Relying on and focusing on the law of attraction to materialize goals is simply one aspect of the challenge. You also need to take action. The Universe pays attention to the ideas and the actions that come from your intentions.

Therefore, if you desire something, show the universe that you are doing all you can to get there. Your actions are the energy behind your intent; it's the gas that fuels the law of attraction. Simply put, it is insufficient to solely concentrate on your intention. You should additionally take action by doing whatever must be done to reach that goal.

It's simple to believe that the Universe hasn't heard you if the law of attraction hasn't worked for you. After that, some people start to think, "Something is wrong with me" or "I can't do it." Those beliefs continue a cycle of negativity and are counterproductive. Negative experiences continue with the assumption that "I assumed positively, and it did not work." Sadly, we can't simply get things; we should balance them with doing something.

Acknowledge your goals, which understandably is easier said than done. But having a plan and putting in the work toward your goals is essential for this law to work. Start by imagining your goals; what does it look and feel like? Once you have a clear picture of what you want, analyze your life to find what isn't working for you anymore.

In this step, it's crucial to recognize passively expecting your goals to just get here because you desire it isn't reality. That presumption is driven by the ego; the work must be done to complete the task.

In my experience, I learned the hard way that my past failed goals were my responsibility, not the Universe's.

Once I decided to dive into my goals. It was this action that led the Universe to see my true potential. I won't bore you with everything I needed to go through, the resources I needed to discover, the risks I needed to take, the ups and downs, and the mistakes I needed to make. But I have to have done something right; I made it and have attracted the things I want; so, can you.

The 369 Method

The 369 technique itself could not be simpler. You write down your manifestation 3 times when you wake up in the morning, 6 times in the afternoon, and then 9 times in the evening. It's that simple! Yet the secret to making your desires a reality is repetition. So, continue exercising the 369-manifestation method every day. Practicing patience is essential if nothing appears to occur after a week, a month, or longer.

While you may not feel like you are making any progress, take a moment to assess any small actions you have taken in the right direction. For example, suppose you want to manifest a romantic partner. In that case, you may think going on several 'meh' dates are a sign of failure when it's not.

Once you start using this technique, you might begin to put yourself out there more. With that one tiny action, you have changed your whole way of thinking by opening yourself up to love and discovering more about yourself and what you desire (or don't) in a partner. After all, enduring the most awful date develops way more self-growth than resting at home.

Importance of 369

If you are not acquainted with numerology, the belief that particular numbers bring their own vibrations and have their own characteristics, these numbers might appear arbitrary. Yet they've been related to good luck and a connection to the universe for years.

Three is a number related to manifestations and the divine. Many who rely on this spiritual technique credit the Greek thinker Pythagoras with its incarnation. Besides the famous Pythagorean theorem, his other trademark credit was his supposed mystical powers in numbers.

According to this theory, the number three is the "noblest of all digits." As for the other two numbers, 6 is related to harmony, a key element in manifestation, and 9 represents the conclusion of a cycle. Below is the value of every number in the series:

- 3 illustrates our connection to resources or the universe and our creative self-expression

- 6 represents our self-confidence and consistency

- 9 represents our internal rebirth; letting go of what no longer serves us and becoming who we end up being

Practicing 369

Every person has their own specific way of writing out their manifestations with this technique. Still, I'll provide you with a few tips for first timers. In my experience, you should be as specific as possible, specifically if what you want has a due date.

Start by thinking of one thing you want to manifest, then write it out in about two sentences. Your desires can be anything, the universe doesn't restrict what you can draw in as long as it doesn't harm you, others, or the planet.

For this approach to work, you need to set aside time every day to write out your manifestations 3 times in the morning when you wake up, then 6 times in the afternoon, and finally 9 times at night before going to bed.

Make sure when you write out your manifestation that it's in the present tense as if what you want is currently yours. Additionally, try to avoid saying "I want" or "I need," these phrases tell the Universe that you aren't in alignment with what you desire, which provides you with more lack of what you want. When you talk like your desires are currently yours, but just haven't shown up yet you're aligning yourself with them.

As I mentioned earlier, don't overly stress over your wants. When and how things get to you isn't something you can control. This is where you need to trust the Universe to give you what you want. Trust that your manifestations will certainly appear exactly when they're meant to.

If you feel negativity or insecurity when trying to manifest using this technique, take some time when uncertainties emerge to take a step back from the approach and take note of them. You have to take time to heal yourself.

Visualization

The power of visualization is your capability to create the desired outcome you don't see. This is because everything ever developed or attained first started as an idea in someone's mind. When you want something, you concentrate your mental power on it. When you have a burning need, this psychological power is intensified by emotions and ultimately manifests in your physical life.

With that said, not every concept is developed like that. To make visualization benefit you (not versus you, as in the case of negative thinking), you need to understand the policies of the mind and the law of attraction.

You can develop whatever you want as soon as you discover the rules of this universal law. The secret is to utilize your creative imagination and visualization for effective outcomes.

So, what's the difference between creativity and visualization? First, you utilize imagination when you develop something in your mind. Then, when you get the information through intuition, you use visualization.

We stay in a globe of diversions. So, every tool is fighting for your interest, guaranteeing approved gratification if you get this or that thing. When the exterior world constantly pesters you, it's nearly impossible to specify your wishes and desires coming from your unique heart. This is when visualization can help you take advantage of your heart's needs and remain positioned with who you are.

One of the most potent benefits of visualization is aiding you to positively affect your frame of mind. Let's consider the advantages of visualization:

- **Get clear on what you desire:** Before you start picturing what you want, you need to understand what it is. Usually, people are wishy-washy when it comes to their goals. Yet visualization helps you mention your desire and work towards them.

- **Boost motivation:** If you recognize what you want, it's tough to fake it till you make it, but this tool will help you. Visualization helps you envision the outcome before it manifests itself in your physical reality and raises your inspiration to work towards accomplishing it.

- **Minimize anxiety:** Visualization, also called mental imagery, is a tested method for stress and anxiety reduction.

  It's extensively exercised as a stand-alone tool or paired with physical leisure methods to assist you in loosening up and achieving a relaxed frame of mind.

- **Come to be even more optimistic:**
  Picturing the procedure of attaining your
  objective creates self-confidence and
  determination as your mind perceives it as an
  authentic experience. In other words, it helps
  you cultivate a sense of calmness you require to
  feel confident and capable.

- **Enhance performance:** In a research study,
  scientists looked at the impact of visualization
  and self-efficacy on athletes' performance.

  They concluded they could obtain the highest
  efficiency with visualization and high self-
  efficacy workouts. Visualization can aid you in
  doing better at any job if you strongly believe in
  yourself.

There are two types of visualization: outcome and
process. I'll go over both of these so you can better
understand them.

- **Outcome visualization:** It's picturing your
  wanted result as an endpoint in the future as if
  it already exists. In other words, you create a
  detailed mental picture of the result using all 5
  senses.
  For example, imagine getting a job offer if your
  goal is to get that job. Then, see yourself
  accepting a call or an email. Next, reflect on
  how you feel in the moment, and think about
  what you see and hear. Finally, make the
  outcome as vivid as possible.

- **Process visualization:** In this type, you envision every step toward accomplishing your goal with all your senses engaged. Using the same example with getting a job offer, imagine being welcomed for a meeting, having a compelling interview, feeling excited, passing the interview, and getting the job.

Here are 6 actions to kick-start your visualization practice.

- Pick what you want. Before you start, you want to clearly understand your preferred outcome.

- Add feelings to the result. Satisfaction differs from one person to another. Therefore, you need to know what happiness is like for you directly.

  You might not know how to get there, but you understand how excellent it feels. So, you want to overlook the how and go straight to sensations. Your inner self understands the best way to bring what you want.

- Include a color. Picture the color connected with the desired outcome. Then, fill your mind with the selected color. The objective is to remove all dark spots and empty areas with the shade. As you do, you eliminate your subconscious blocks.

- Make it brighter. Your chosen shade represents the energy of your goal, so you want to make it as bright as possible to magnify it.

- Envision possible problems and how you handle them quickly and gracefully as you progress toward your objective.

- Think of the next easiest step you can take to make your wanted result happen. Take that action.

- Use the present tense to write your preferred result on an index card. Then, review it in the early morning and in the evening.

How to Create a Vision Board

Creating a vision board is a great tool that allows you to enter and use your power to manifest in a unique way. This method helps you figure out exactly how you want your life to look and what you want in it. This approach enables us to claim aloud that we are prepared to develop or get our dreams and collaborate with universal laws to create our reality. When you create a vision board it's a charming, alchemical procedure filled with sensation, activities, pictures, and words. So, if you're new to making vision boards now is a terrific time to make your first one. I am excited to teach you the general method I use to make my vision boards.

Do a standing check and evaluation. The first thing I do is take a seat with my journal and review what has been happening in my life. I take the time to reflect on what's happened in my life, especially over the past year. Then, I look at everything from the goals I successfully achieved, to the things that didn't go my way and taught me a lesson, and lastly what made me happy.

Set and prioritize your goals. Next, I get something to write with, you can use pen and paper or write it out on your phone. I then think about and write down my goals, this can be the things I want to accomplish in the next year or the next five years.

This step is basically a brain dump that consists of every little thing from my large goals and dreams to my little wants. For example, I might want to get a new car this year, pick up a new hobby, or just want my year to be focused on happiness.

After the very first mind dump, I review my notes and ideas to determine what I need to do. Then, I circle the most important items on the list and create a new list if needed. I ask myself, what are things I want? The things I deem necessary will 100% make it onto my vision board. I ensure that my big goals have a place to go on my board, of course, smaller goals and wants still get a place. I just work them around what I'm prioritizing for the year.

Find photos, words, and sayings for your vision board. In this step look for pictures, words, and anything else that represents your goals. One way I do this is by looking through old magazines to find something that represents my goal. Also, if there's nothing in the magazine that speaks to me about one of the things I want to accomplish, I'll do a Google search and print one out. I rely on the net a great deal nowadays to find engaging photos to represent my goals.

In this stage, I often have a lot more pictures than I need or will use, which gives me a great opportunity to make my board look the way I want it. Given that I have a plethora of images, I take time to go through my stack to find the best options.

When I do this, I am trying to find several photos that capture each purpose's significance and feeling. My finished vision boards include a mix of photos, words, and sayings I find in magazines and those I print from the web.

Come up with sections to structure your vision board. You don't have to do this part, but I found that it helps me, and I really like it. Usually, I create sections of my poster board. Sometimes I draw lines to form a space for each area of my life such as finances, relationships, career, etc.

Doing this provides an excellent framework and keeps your general life goal classifications well-rounded. After creating my sections and liking the way they look, I'll write my intentions and goals in the section it belongs in. It doesn't matter how the writing looks and what exactly you write since it'll get covered up later.

Plan your vision board. If you didn't do the last step place your cutouts where you want them in a way that looks good to you without gluing them on your poster board. But if you did do the last step, take your stack of pictures, and place them in the correct sections. If you like, cut backgrounds away or move pictures as you go.

You don't have to use all your pictures on your board, if you want you can save some for future use. Once you're done placing everything on the board, take a step back to look at how you arranged it. Ask yourself, do I like how it looks? Does it show what I want to accomplish? If you are more than satisfied with the board, continue to the following step.

Glue your pictures down. Now that you are happy with your picture placements, you can start to glue them down.

Work with one word or picture at a time to ensure your vision board comes out exactly how you want. Smooth out each piece with your hands as much as possible to prevent wrinkling.

Decorate as you like. This is one more optional step; however, it's a creative way to complete your vision board. You can write, doodle, or draw around the collaged photos.

You can use pens, markers, or glitter to add your own flare. Additionally, you can use collage products such as bangles, shoelaces, ribbons, or whatever else you prefer.

Daily Rituals for Connections

To connect with your board daily, it's vital to display your board where you will see it often. You can put it in your office, bedroom, or living room. If you don't want to mount it to your wall, you can take a picture of the vision board or create an electronic duplicate and set it as your phone or computer's background.

Then use your vision board to build a plan to start working toward your desires. Your vision board should be a guide to your preferred life. There are numerous methods to do this, such as:

- Review your board as you work toward your goals to see how far you've come.

- Get a journal and reflect on the goals on your board; consider how you are working toward them.

- Close your eyes and imagine yourself accomplishing your goals, and how it makes you feel.

Gratitude Attraction Boosters

As you end your manifestation session, add a "thank you, Universe, for offering this to me." at the end of it or any comparable message that makes sense with what you wrote. With this added 'thank you ahead of time, you are reaffirming your confidence in attracting what you want. This stirs your positivity and vigorously changes things in your favor.

Do not hesitate to say "thank you" more than once if it helps. State it 5 times. 10 times. 100 times. Whatever you like. Try it as soon as possible, and you'll understand its value.

As you detail each thing, you are grateful for, feel free to include reasons why you are thankful. For example, it's convenient and adequate to say, "I am so pleased and happy about my promotion." However, you can go deeper and say, "I am so pleased and happy for my new promotion since the additional pay adds more comfort to my life.

In addition, the larger office with the added large windows allows a lot of sunlight in and truly keeps me in an excellent state of mind."

If you have the time, include it in your everyday routine. In that case, this option helps make every session much more durable and delightful. It also gives you something even more to expect the next day.

As you go over your gratitude list, magnify the power and sensation of your thankfulness by imagining your gratitude shaking outside your body as a ray of warm light. The light can be white, gold, or any bright shade that feels excellent.

This light is your method of offering positivity, love, and recovery energy to the entire world around you. You are saying thanks to everyone for improving your life by making points much better for everything around you. You'll be surprised at how much happy you usually feel as you do this.

Scripting Method

Scripting is a powerful writing technique used to assist you in materializing anything you desire, from having an excellent mood throughout the day to getting your dream house.

When you script, you discuss precisely what you want in your life as if it's occurring or has occurred. Think of scripting as a written form of visualization. Instead of shutting your eyes and imagining what you desire, you write out all that information.

Writing out this information lets you get details about what you want and feel what it's like to have it. By thinking and feeling what it's like to have what you want, you start to bring those things into your life.

Scripting can be done for anything in your life, big or small. For example, you can write about a dream trip, a job you want, something you want to buy, a business idea, or even simply define how you desire your day to go. All you have to do is get a pen and paper and comply with the actions listed below!

How to Script

Clear your mind.

Before you begin creating, sit silently and breathe for a couple of minutes. Do your best to clear your mind and be completely present in the moment. If things stand out in your mind, like the order of business or concerns, set them to the side.

Then, go back to concentrating on your breath for another minute or two. This will give you a clear, fresh sense when you begin to script.

Those who currently practice meditation likely know the power of the sensation of a clear mind operating on a high vibration. However, for those who haven't yet experienced this, begin including short reflection practices into your day, consisting of gratefulness, to aid you in quickly slipping into a positive frame of mind.

After taking deep breaths for a few minutes, I like to compose a paragraph of points I am grateful for before starting to script. This assists me in entering a much more favorable state of mind and afterward networking that thankfulness in the direction of what I am manifesting.

Select what you are going to script about.

The wonderful thing about scripting is you can do it for literally anything, your approaching day, future objectives, or a specific item you want to have. So, you can pick a broad topic, like exactly how you'd like the coming week to go, or focus on a specific subject, like manifesting your dream house or partner.

To begin, choose one thing to script about. For example, if you have an important day or just want a good one, you can write exactly how you would like it to go.

You can define how you go about your day, how you feel, and how things go. Then, picture everything working out just as you desire it to. An important note is that you are writing what you want to happen, not what you don't want.

Select the tense for your writing.

A usual manifestation blunder is discussing what you desire in the future tense. However, if you are constantly wanting, you'll continue to bring in ideas and points that will maintain you in that state. To attract what you prefer into your life, discussing it like you already have it, is essential. So, a fundamental part of scripting is using present or past tense to write your manifestations.

When you sit down to write, pick whichever tense feels better to you. For example, it may be best to write in the here and now as if it's happening in present moment. You can see it unfolding around you, or you can write in the past tense as if it already happened and all the emotions you felt while it was occurring.

Add lots of details, the more the better.

Then, as you compose, get specific details of what you desire. Include as much information as possible and keep pushing your mind to think of more.

 This will certainly aid you in getting clear about what you want and assist you in writing like it's currently yours. Here are some questions to help you with adding details when you are scripting:

- What does it look like? What size, color, and style does it have?
- What specific functions does it have?
- Where are you?
- Does it have a sound?
- Is there a specific smell?

- How does it feel to have it?
- When you hold it, how do you feel?
- After realizing it's yours, how do you feel?

Reread your scripts.

After you've made scripting a habit, take time to examine what you've scripted about and highlight each item that's come true.

It's fun to do and will assist in reinforcing your idea in the law of attraction. If there are parts of your script that have not manifested yet, don't stop believing. Instead, rely on the universe and understand that what you desire or something better is headed your way.

Chapter 5: Present is Perfect

On my journey with the law of attraction, one of the most essential spiritual rules I learned is that the present is perfect. Most people have heard of this rule before. However, the majority of individuals don't fully understand it.

How can today be ideal when you are sick or have a busted leg? How can the here and now be exceptional when you have colossal debt? Can today be superb when your sweetheart just broke up with you? It certainly doesn't look or feel excellent in any of these scenarios.

Though I've had my fair share of student loan debt, this financial burden was ideal because it required me to manage the facts regarding my expenses. Until I found out exactly how to meet my much deeper demands, I would continue to spend too much. When I obtained my need to be cherished and satisfied, investing passed my means quite naturally.

Suppose you can identify that today is ideal; in that case, you'll be much calmer when handling life's relatively "adverse" stuff.

Overall, it can be hard to see the good in bad situations while they are happening. So, it's important to reflect on the things in your life to try and see the good.

Unlocking the Now

Whatever you are doing, from eating to scrolling your phone, you need to be mindful of what you are doing. For example, just how frequently are you eating your lunch while watching television at the same time?

This means you could distance yourself from what you are doing and not live in the moment because all of your attention isn't on that task at hand.

Another way to live in the moment is to write a daily list of things you are grateful for. Then, write at least three big things you are thankful for in your life. After that, you can do a gratitude rampage, where you compose as many things as you can think of in a set amount of time.

While it might feel much more practical to multitask on more than one thing at once, regularly handling multiple tasks makes it difficult to be mindful.

While doing something that requires your complete attention can appear overwhelming initially, recognize how much extra productive you are when fully participating in a task.

Compare this with trying to press numerous things into one time period or spending half of your energy on three various functions.

Align with Your Manifestation

One guaranteed way to understand that your energy is divided is by the existence of negative thoughts and unpleasant feelings. A part of you wants what you want, and another doubts your capacity to create it. Split energy not only feels horrible; it blocks our ability to attract every one of the blessings we've asked for.

Split power is what you experience when the powerful energy of your wish is opposed or blocked by some inconsistent power.

For example, the contradictory power may develop from thinking about a time when things didn't go your way or seeing your life through the lens of absence or insufficiency.

The good news is you were born receptive, relying on, and open to receiving the Universe's wealth. So, you can learn to strengthen your power to align with your manifestations. We simply have to stop participating in the habits of an idea that splits our energy.

We straighten ourselves with those realities by thinking regarding them and, for that reason feeding them with our energy. To align your energy with any type of preferred result, like ease, wealth, and pleasure, you first must uncover what you are presently aligned with.

You were born with an innate capability to align your energy with the adequate power that creates and sustains this world.

Heart Mind Sync

Relaxing from social media sites and various other technologies can additionally aid you in remaining even more present-focused. However, while you could think that using social media is helping you stay attached to the world, it negatively affects your ability to be mindful.

Regular exercise or even a stroll in the park can aid you in staying more concentrated on your present tasks. Including yoga as part of your daily routine is another terrific way to sync your mind and body, particularly if it's coupled with reflection and mindfulness exercises.

If you can't make time for yoga classes, simply stopping what you are doing to take a couple of minutes for some standard positions can help you come back into the moment.

In particular, when you are with other individuals, you can try concentrating on the people and the setting around you instead of being sidetracked by your phone.

Putting in the time to sit and do some deep breathing will help you focus your mind on connecting with your body. In addition, taking slow, controlled breaths helps prevent feelings of panic and other negative thoughts from taking over. It also allows for more control during the activity in which you are currently engaged. One straight forward and quick method to try is the 4-7-8 breathing technique.

Getting Out of Your Way

Our ideas are assumed realities. They are our inner declarations regarding ourselves. However, they have shaped us, probably unknown to many of us; they have been with us since childhood. These generalizations come to be deeply inserted in our subconscious and materialize as restricting ideas that affect much of what we assume, claim, and do.

When we allow our lives to be formed by these limiting beliefs, the behaviors we take on enhance our thoughts. Therefore, we become specialists in developing our self-fulfilling revelations.

Picked up nearly by osmosis from those that have had the most significant impact on us in our developmental years. So, our self-limiting ideas are like a covert undertone that has affected who we are today.

They usually develop in our formative years in reaction to painful experiences. Through these experiences, we build our own, typically manipulated generalization of life. Self-limiting beliefs are the ones that have the best capacity to influence you negatively to hinder your real-life possibilities.

Therefore, we create restricting ideas to safeguard us from future pain. The great news is that, on the other hand, it's also possible to let go of these old beliefs and establish new ones to produce a more favorable story for ourselves.

Identify any type of self-limiting beliefs and what behaviors they have led to.

First, think about your limiting beliefs, then select one or two to focus on and attempt to reflect on the detrimental influence of these beliefs on your practices. For example, how you lead your school and connect with others.

By acknowledging how these beliefs materialize themselves in us, we accumulate a self-awareness that enables us to be even more prepared when they conveniently re-occur in our life.

When we can detect and name these ideas and behaviors, we have taken the first step to produce a new story with our new beliefs.

Consider where these ideas could have originated from.

By looking into the origin of our thoughts and questioning them, we can become aware that the proof we have used to validate these ideas is flawed, restricted, or circumstantial.

In turn, we can begin to break the structures of these ideas. First, review what the source(s) of these beliefs could be. In some cases, it can be communications you had about a specific event in the past that has aided in creating these ideas.

Review circumstances where these beliefs have been revealed to be incorrect.

By re-evaluating the "evidence," we can start to redress this equilibrium and perhaps realize that we haven't been fair to ourselves. At the same time, we can overlook instances that would act as proof versus our self-limiting ideas, e.g., when we have handled conflicts well.

So, a vital next step when tackling self-limiting thoughts is to consider all the times that these beliefs have been proven inaccurate.

Explore what ideas might much better sustain you as a leader and person.

To do so, it's best to ask yourself what type of behaviors you wish to exhibit as a leader (and as an individual) and then work backward to what ideas might help you do this.

This direction will certainly be essential in keeping you concentrated as you attempt to create brand-new beliefs and create brand-new behaviors.

Challenge your thoughts.

The most straight forward point is to claim "quit" when you feel these self-limiting voices in your head or find yourself exhibiting old practices. Where possible, consciously look to customize or challenge this with an extra verifying statement such as "I can be organized." If this feels a bit much, modify this statement to recognize that you are growing.

This can be the most challenging bit, as it's likely that these behaviors are entrenched and are bound to show up whether you want them to or not.

Therefore, as you look to establish new practices, you must strive to respond to the old behaviors and ideas when they re-appear (which they will).

This indicates carefully enjoying your conduct and thought processes and attempting to respond to and change these.

Creating new practices, practice as well as reinforcement.

The final step is to carry out activities straightened to the new patterns you want to develop. Seek methods and tools to assist you if you wish to establish ways of being more ordered.

Practicing this, and making minor adjustments, gradually can cause significant adjustments to your thought processes, hence your narrative and, subsequently, your behavior and management.

As we do this, we must recognize that (like our pupils), we also require time, persistence, and understanding as we undertake this understanding and growth.

Presence Energy - The Never-Changing Nature of Your Being

As the law of attraction discusses that our authentic self is constantly increasing and becoming extra as a result of living life. Concentrating on how we want to feel or what we wish to experience in the future brings us into higher positioning with the visibility of our true selves.

Existence can also be enhanced by changing any inconsistent beliefs we might have. In the absence of contradictory opinions, we would typically have the presence of our genuine selves.

We are constantly present, but our experience of life depends on the degree we are mentally present. This may explain how much energy or awareness of the wider non-physical part of ourselves we are enabling to stream with us at any moment.

When we mentally exist, we have a more profound and prosperous life experience. Life feels much more meaningful; we think of our link to everyone and every little thing, we feel sustained, and more of what is desired materializes. In addition, when we are in a state of presence, it positively influences those around us.

Reflection helps raise presence as it attaches us a lot more with our true selves by distracting us from any kind of not-good thoughts. The existence of our authentic self is always there for us, but we have to be on the ideal frequency to experience it.

Regularly, using the law of attraction over time, we will continue to experience more of the existence of our actual selves.

Lastly, concentrating on what we appreciate in our current life will increase our existence as this tune us to the frequency of our authentic selves, which is in a state of admiration and seeing the best in everyone and everything.

Meditation and the law of attraction

From the outside, a person meditating may appear to be breathing or repeating a sound or expression. Inside their brain, nevertheless, it's a different tale. Modern diagnostic and imaging methods show that meditation can favorably influence your mind and psychological wellness.

The practice of reflection is countless years old, and different types originate from all over the world. However, modern-day science has only started studying this technique in detail.

Some of the most significant jumps in scientific research's understanding of meditation have been possible thanks to modern-day innovation.

Meditation is a technique that entails concentrating or clearing your mind using a combination of psychological and physical methods. Depending on your selected meditation, you can meditate to relax, lower anxiety, stress, and more.

The law of attraction runs based on your unconscious mind. The objective is to acknowledge persisting patterns as rapidly as possible, so you can understand your internal concerns and work on healing them. A large part of cleaning up what you bring in externally is to familiarize you with what you have going on internally.

Think of your conscious mind, your "thinking" mind, as the ship's captain. When the aware mind informs you to enter particular instructions and your ship slams into the rocks, it implies the ship's team is breaking the captain's orders. It suggests an incongruence between what the captain is directing and what the team is doing.

Integrating Mindfulness

Your thoughts and activities develop an outcome. Everything you think, claim, and do will have a result. Every action creates a force of energy that goes back to its kind, and power continues to flow back and forth.

When things aren't working out, consider the law of attraction because it brings you energies that reflect what's happening inside you. So, this is the best time to concentrate on what you are drawing to yourself and develop a way of interrupting negative thoughts.

Meditation for the Law of Attraction

Start by analyzing one pattern at a time and notice how this theme has been present in your life. Take notice of limiting beliefs and negative thoughts that lead to your negative feelings.

Ask your higher self to help determine if your patterns contribute to any unwanted circumstances.

What was happening at that time? What was your environment like? Then, ask questions determining how your inner world was affecting your external world. Now, make the intention to heal old wounds and let go of the thoughts that no longer serve you. You can even ask the Universe to send you healing energy.

Then visualize the person, belief, or pattern you are ready to let go of. Picture flowing this healing energy from your heart to what you are trying to heal. Additionally, say what you need to say in order to complete this task. You can ask for guidance or say a symbolic poem to cut ties.

Now, focus on what you want to attract into your life and visualize it in the most brilliant, colorful, and exciting way. Then, pretend it has already happened and notice how you are feeling. Once your visualization feels real and powerful, take a deep breath. On the exhale, breathe life into the image; blow into it as much as you can.

The law of attraction works according to your subconscious mind, where all your ideas, memories, experiences, and goals are kept. So doing this visualization uses both your conscious and unconscious minds, bringing them into placement to help you actualize your deepest needs and intents.

Remain focused on this visualization as you reside in a place of thankfulness, inspiration, and abundance. Remember that Rome wasn't built overnight and that a day-to-day method anchors you to the fascinating aspects of who you are and attracts limitless possibilities.

Power of Meditation for Attracting What You Want

Suppose you chat with one individual who loves math and another who hates math. In that case, they'll each have a different understanding of math. How you view and translate your truth will undoubtedly result in what you attract in your life.

Since the law of attraction is about what you are producing, let's speak about the concept of truth for a moment. Truth is an assumption. It's an analysis. What one person thinks to be genuine may not hold true for a different person.

Creating Your Own Meditation Technique

Merely follow the steps listed below, and you will end up with your own meditation method that you can utilize whenever you need to.

Determine what you want to get out of it:

Why are you creating your own meditation technique? There are many different reasons people practice meditation. List the feelings you want to have from your meditation. In this step don't add a long list of varying emotions, you can always create an additional meditation for various reasons later on.

Compose one or two points you desire to get out of the reflection. It might be a feeling like joy, or it could be something extra concrete like you hope to make a new friend.

Decide what qualities you intend to cultivate:

If you want to grow a particular feeling like happiness, you already understand the high quality you need. In this situation, you can proceed to the following step. If you are attempting to obtain something concrete from this, then you'll need to create your required qualities. Ask yourself, what qualities do I need to reach my goals?

Remember moments when you had those high qualities:

Your memories consist of energy you can use. Think about some of your memories associated with the qualities you are looking for. When you think of your memories, attempt to focus on the exact facet of the memory that makes you satisfied.

For example, was it a person's smile, or possibly a scent or a specific noise in the memory that contains positive emotions for you? Write those points down.

To make your meditation a lot more powerful, concentrate on those memories. What was it regarding those memories that made you feel so good?

Wrap-up: By now, you've written down what you want to attain, the qualities you need to accomplish it, and the memories associated with times when you had those qualities.

You need these points before you create your meditation technique, so make sure you have them written.

Time to create your meditation:

Let's examine how to produce your own meditation. Like with many reflections, merely shut your eyes, and focus your mind on your breathing.

Now work your way through the list of memories you created above. You will undoubtedly feel remarkable when you make it to the end of your list of memories.

Benefits of Meditation

The Mayo Clinic states that meditation is an easy, quick way to minimize anxiety. At the same time, many professionals believe that you can't find a better, natural means with no side impacts, to manage stress and anxiety than through a meditation technique. Some benefits of meditation are:

- **Anxiousness.** Mindfulness meditation has expanded in appeal recently and might help decrease anxiety. Yale recently published a study comparing breathing reflection to mindfulness for managing stress and anxiety.

- **Rest.** When it pertains to any health-related worry, physicians will constantly ask if you are getting adequate rest and about the quality of your sleep.

  According to SleepFoundation.org, sleeping disorders are a common rest issue for adults. They specify, that meditation can boost your quality of sleep and reduce discomfort.

- **Blood pressure.** Another benefit of mindfulness meditation and mantra techniques is the natural lowering of blood pressure. Still, it might call for everyday meditation to see continued advantages.

- **Heart wellness.** Just as high blood pressure is a significant contributor to fatality, heart disease is the cause of death in over a half-million lives annually in the United States.

  That's one in four deaths. Multiple meditation types get us out of a fight or flight response and lower our heart rate to reduce our risk of heart disease.

The Mindful Brain

Just as there are several physical benefits to meditation, there are many fantastic mental wellness advantages of meditation. So, let's continue considering a few advantages connected to the mind and well-being.

- **Emotional health.** Scientists found enhanced degrees of appreciation, self-worth, positive outlook, joviality, serenity, complete life satisfaction, and quality of life in individuals as early as day one of starting a meditation practice.

- **Self-awareness and intuition.** Just as reflection has a practical side, it can additionally have a spiritual side. From the beginning of time, yogis have practiced meditating for more significant states of awareness.

Scientists generally agree that humans only utilize about 30% of their capacity. Meditation is one way of increasing that capacity.

Therefore, along with self-awareness and intuition, several additionally use meditation to materialize their needs and goals.

- **Memory.** Scientific research on a health and wellness epidemic is expected to influence 40% of all baby boomers, consisting of exactly how meditation may enhance brain health and lower 5 of the 6 significant threats elements for Alzheimer's and dementia.

Meditation and Self-Limiting Belief

In these ways, meditation can serve as an effective device to assist you in surpassing your limiting beliefs. In addition, practicing regularly will undoubtedly open the door to a world without limits.

Meditation is a cleanser of your consciousness. When you enter the space between your thoughts, you go into the area of absolute, unbounded, pure consciousness.

This is a domain of recognition that is beyond and immune to all types of contamination. Negative thoughts, hostility, worry, question, and other limiting mental constructs cannot hold up against the new light of pure unity awareness.

You recognize that every person is a collection of countless ideas, and from each distinct perspective, they are beneficial. Therefore, the concept of needing to push one narrative over others is an ineffective and usually meaningless use of your energy.

Meditation stands as a distinctively effective device to change or transcend limiting beliefs. Through its standard technique, reflection begins to gradually dig deep into those ideas that no longer support you and make room for something brand-new and more helpful.

As the mind settles down right into quieter levels of its awareness, the subconscious loops you've been battling for years end up being much less important in your meditation. In the past, you could have felt urged to strictly protect your ideas and opinions, probably in a protective manner.

However, with the calm tranquility of reflection, the urge to voice your point of sight decreases, and the top quality of defenselessness emerge in your awareness.

The limiting beliefs you knowingly or automatically harbor are at some point consumed in the fire of more significant states of awareness. Then, as you start to understand your true nature as a pure boundless spirit, the entire concept of restrictions and borders starts to dissolve.

Ultimately, you are freed from all tightness into a state of increased understanding.

By its very nature, meditation is a technique to go beyond or go past the turbulence of your thinking process. In doing this frequently, you likewise start bypassing the crusty, old, and outworn ideas you lug around with you daily.

The more often you do this, the more your limiting beliefs begin to shed their grip on you and are much less likely to influence your actions in unfavorable methods.

Meditations

When we practice meditation, we infuse durable and far-ranging advantages right into our lives. As a plus, you don't need additional devices or an expensive membership. While meditation isn't a wonder drug, it can help in some much-needed areas in your life.

Periodically, that's all we need to make better options for ourselves, our families, and our lives. Among the most important devices, you can bring to your meditation technique are a little persistence, some compassion for yourself, as well as a comfortable location to sit.

Getting Started

Starting your meditation practice is less complex than most people assume. To start, sit somewhere quiet and relaxing. Then set a timer for as long as you want, but it'll be easier if you work your way up longer sessions.

Notice your body and your breath as you try not to move from your chosen spot. Don't be discouraged if your mind wanders; it takes time to learn to stay present.

Finally, end your session with kindness and note how you feel, and the world around you. That's it! You concentrate your attention, if your mind wanders bring it back to the present moment as kindly as possible, and as often as you need.

Health

There are several sorts of meditation, including, transcendental reflection, which is a method that enables your mind to focus inward, remaining alert to various other ideas or experiences without allowing them to interfere.

Mindfulness reflection may use an item of emphasis, such as ringing a bell, chanting, touching beads, or staring at a picture. Relocating meditation consists of qi gong, Tai Chi, and yoga.

Gradually increase the amount of time you try to meditate. If you are unsure how to get started, look for online courses on meditation, get suggestions from pals, or study various types that fascinate you.

Wealth and Abundance

If you claim things like, I have plenty, and I have more than enough, you will undoubtedly experience just that. Meditation is the path to feeling wealth and abundance. Meditation helps you release stress and anxiety. When these adverse emotions disappear, you will be open to feeling your inherent positivity.

You remain in a place where you can get positivity all around. Just when you welcome and encourage good ideas, they will undoubtedly flow. That is why you can use meditation to feel abundance and wealth.

It develops that space within you. If you concentrate on negative thoughts, you will just feel negativity. But, on the other hand, if you experience, value, and embrace positivity, you will undoubtedly feel full of it.

Love and Relationship

Showing and receiving love and kindness through multiple relationship types provides us with a needed and proficient remedy to negative mental states. Which may be merely too strong to attend to through straight thought.

At such times, formal love and kindness meditation techniques can soften one's negative mind to ensure we can avoid succumbing to their powers in our relationships.

When love arises spontaneously throughout the mindfulness method, just calling or focusing on loving qualities makes your meditation practice relationship specific which assists us in acknowledging the qualities in our life. It'll also direct our minds and heart in the direction of loving relationships, specifically in hard times.

Rise Above Fear

This is where reflection can be found in. It's when our concern for particular situations, like the anxiety of the unknown, takes root. So, when we are looking to meditate to get over anxiety, it is essential to first recognize that many of our concerns identify with an earlier time in our life, an imagined horror, or a stressful experience.

Whether we are kids or adults, shining some light on our worries is the first step toward managing them. "The more you try to reduce concern, either by ignoring it or doing another thing to displace it, the more you will experience it," stated Kristy Dalrymple, a medical aide teacher of psychiatry and human behavior.

Anxiety is something we might have lived with for a long time. When we practice meditation, we embark on a journey to a calmer, less reactive, and less fearful mind. In relaxing, we not only quell our anxieties but also raise the possibility of overcoming them. It takes method and patience to unwind and understand fear to the degree that it no longer has a hold over us.

Embrace Love

With practice, meditation comes to be the personification of love and empathy all on its own, capable of welcoming any type of mental state. It also allows us to see, recognize, and accept open-hearted non-reactive, non-judgmental love.

At the same time, we can see right into the nature of the rage or pain we feel for whatever it is. Meditation that embraces love undermines, deteriorates, and vaporizes; our anger similar to touching a soap bubble. Once we get to that place, we come out of it embracing love itself developing from extended silence, without an invite because it's within us.

Affirmations

Many people think that affirmations are impractical wishful thinking. However, affirmations are like a repetitive workout you would do to enhance your health and wellness.

These positive sayings are basically exercise for our minds and our expectation should be an improvement of our mental state. The positive psychological phrases we use can change the way we think which will help us in time, to start believing and acting more positively.

There have been several studies to prove the effectiveness of affirmations. These studies concluded that when we have a strong sense of self respect for ourselves it boosts our health.

So, as an example, if you want to be healthier but are worried because the way you eat and the amount of exercise aren't helping you reach your goals, utilize positive affirmations. When you reflect on your values it'll spur a change in your behavior and allow you to get to where you want.

In addition, improving your sense of self-affirmations likewise helps us to lessen the results of tension. Affirmations are declaration statements that allow you to challenge and get rid of unfavorable and self-sabotaging ideas. Then, you can start making positive adjustments when you consistently repeat and believe.

Lastly, mental health professionals use affirmations to efficiently help individuals with anxiety, low self-confidence, and similar mental health issues. Also, these positive statements have been revealed to boost the section of our minds that make us most likely to make positive adjustments about our wellness.

Writing Out Affirmations

When you compose your affirmations use the past or present tense. The idea is to speak and create a positive phrase as if it's happening or has already happened. Additionally, make sure you add feeling to your statements because they become much more reliable if they have emotional weight.

For example, "I am well-rehearsed, well-prepared, and I can give a terrific presentation" is a terrific affirmation to use if you are nervous about public speaking.

You need to desire this adjustment to take place, so when you choose an affirmation, you want to repeat it so that it is meaningful to you. Make a note of several areas or habits that you'd like to deal with.

Then, ensure they work with the qualities, values, and things you want to work on. Choosing issues that are important to you will help you feel motivated to accomplish your goals.

Determine the places in your life that you would like to change. Would you have a more productive day?

However, it's important to write sensible affirmations because they aren't magic spells.

As an example, if you are not happy with how much you get paid. You can use affirmations to raise your self-confidence to ask for a raise. If you repeatedly think something like, "I am not talented enough to progress in my career," it'll turn into a self-fulfilling prophecy.

So, change this statement into a good affirmation such as, "I am an experienced and knowledgeable specialist progressing in my career."

Practice turning negatives into positives on your journey. If you are dealing with negative thoughts and self-talk, write the relentless ideas that are troubling you. Then, choose an affirmation that is the reverse of that idea.

Affirmation declarations target specific problems you have including behaviors, patterns, and ideas you are fighting with. Focusing on the qualities you want to build can aid you in creating an affirmation declaration that fits your requirements.

Boost Confidence with Affirmation

Self-esteem has to do with how you feel about yourself. It implies you feel good enough on your own without having to be validated by others. We feel best when we are confident, beneficial, and less worried.

Therefore, utilizing affirmations in your everyday routine will certainly assist in boosting your self-esteem.

Some affirmations you can try to boost your confidence are:

- I love myself for who I have become
- I am valuable to myself and others
- I am grateful to be me
- I value myself
- I look fondly upon memories of my past
- I have a bright future filled with success
- I deserve to take a break and relax
- I am happy with who I am
- I deserve happiness and embrace it

Conclusion

Thank you for making it through to the end of this book. Let's hope it was informative and provided you with all the tools you need to achieve your goals, whatever they may be. The next step is to start practicing the law of attraction and the different tips to help boost your manifestations. Some steps that you can take to help you use the law of attraction in your life include:

- Be grateful
- Learn to recognize negative reasoning and combat it
- Envision your objectives
- Use positive affirmations
- Try to find the positives in all circumstances
- Reframe bad occasions in a more positive way

While the law of attraction might not be an on-the-spot solution for all situations, it can aid you in a more assured view of life. It'll additionally allow you to remain to be stimulated to paint the life of your dreams. Finally, if you found this book helpful, please leave a review on Amazon; it's always appreciated!

Journal

I want to manifest ____
My affirmation:

3 affirmations in the morning

____
____
____

6 affirmations in the afternoon

____
____
____
____
____
____

9 affirmations in the evening

____
____
____
____
____
____
____
____
____

Today I am grateful for?

____
____
____

I want to manifest ________________________________
My affirmation:

3 affirmations in the morning

---

6 affirmations in the afternoon

---

9 affirmations in the evening

Today I am grateful for?

I want to manifest ____
My affirmation:

3 affirmations in the morning

____

____

____

6 affirmations in the afternoon

____

____

____

____

____

____

9 affirmations in the evening

____

____

____

____

____

____

____

____

____

Today I am grateful for?

____

____

____

____

I want to manifest ___________________________________
My affirmation:

3 affirmations in the morning

____

____

____

6 affirmations in the afternoon

____

____

____

____

____

____

9 affirmations in the evening

____

____

____

____

____

____

____

____

____

Today I am grateful for?

____

____

____

____

I want to manifest ________________
My affirmation:

3 affirmations in the morning

6 affirmations in the afternoon

9 affirmations in the evening

Today I am grateful for?

I want to manifest ______________________________
My affirmation:

3 affirmations in the morning

____

____

____

6 affirmations in the afternoon

____

____

____

____

____

____

9 affirmations in the evening

____

____

____

____

____

____

____

____

____

Today I am grateful for?

____

____

____

____

I want to manifest ____
My affirmation:

3 affirmations in the morning

____

____

____

6 affirmations in the afternoon

____

____

____

____

____

____

9 affirmations in the evening

____

____

____

____

____

____

____

____

____

Today I am grateful for?

____

____

____

____

I want to manifest ______________________________
My affirmation:

3 affirmations in the morning

____

____

____

6 affirmations in the afternoon

____

____

____

____

____

____

9 affirmations in the evening

____

____

____

____

____

____

____

____

____

Today I am grateful for?

____

____

____

____

I want to manifest ______________________________
My affirmation:

3 affirmations in the morning

6 affirmations in the afternoon

9 affirmations in the evening

Today I am grateful for?

I want to manifest ________________________________
My affirmation:

3 affirmations in the morning

____

____

____

6 affirmations in the afternoon

____

____

____

____

____

____

9 affirmations in the evening

____

____

____

____

____

____

____

____

____

Today I am grateful for?

____

____

____

____

I want to manifest ____
My affirmation:

3 affirmations in the morning

6 affirmations in the afternoon

9 affirmations in the evening

Today I am grateful for?

I want to manifest _______________________________________
My affirmation:

3 affirmations in the morning

____

____

____

6 affirmations in the afternoon

____

____

____

____

____

____

9 affirmations in the evening

____

____

____

____

____

____

____

____

____

Today I am grateful for?

____

____

____

____

I want to manifest ________________________________
My affirmation:

3 affirmations in the morning

____

____

____

6 affirmations in the afternoon

____

____

____

____

____

____

9 affirmations in the evening

____

____

____

____

____

____

____

____

____

Today I am grateful for?

____

____

____

____

____

I want to manifest ______________________________
My affirmation:

3 affirmations in the morning

____

____

____

6 affirmations in the afternoon

____

____

____

____

____

____

9 affirmations in the evening

____

____

____

____

____

____

____

____

____

Today I am grateful for?

____

____

____

____

I want to manifest _______________________________
My affirmation:

3 affirmations in the morning

6 affirmations in the afternoon

9 affirmations in the evening

Today I am grateful for?

I want to manifest ______________________________
My affirmation:

3 affirmations in the morning

____

____

____

6 affirmations in the afternoon

____

____

____

____

____

____

9 affirmations in the evening

____

____

____

____

____

____

____

____

____

Today I am grateful for?

____

____

____

____

I want to manifest ____
My affirmation:

3 affirmations in the morning

6 affirmations in the afternoon

9 affirmations in the evening

Today I am grateful for?

I want to manifest ________________________________
My affirmation:

3 affirmations in the morning

____

____

____

6 affirmations in the afternoon

____

____

____

____

____

9 affirmations in the evening

____

____

____

____

____

____

____

____

Today I am grateful for?

____

____

____

____

I want to manifest ________________________________
My affirmation:

<u>3 affirmations in the morning</u>

____

____

____

<u>6 affirmations in the afternoon</u>

____

____

____

____

____

____

<u>9 affirmations in the evening</u>

____

____

____

____

____

____

____

____

____

<u>Today I am grateful for?</u>

____

____

____

____

____

I want to manifest _______________________________
My affirmation:

3 affirmations in the morning

____

____

____

6 affirmations in the afternoon

____

____

____

____

____

____

9 affirmations in the evening

____

____

____

____

____

____

____

____

____

Today I am grateful for?

____

____

____

____

I want to manifest ___________________________________
My affirmation:

3 affirmations in the morning

____

____

____

6 affirmations in the afternoon

____

____

____

____

____

____

9 affirmations in the evening

____

____

____

____

____

____

____

____

____

Today I am grateful for?

____

____

____

____

I want to manifest _______________________________
My affirmation:

3 affirmations in the morning

6 affirmations in the afternoon

9 affirmations in the evening

Today I am grateful for?

I want to manifest ____

My affirmation:

3 affirmations in the morning

6 affirmations in the afternoon

9 affirmations in the evening

Today I am grateful for?

I want to manifest _______________________________
My affirmation:

3 affirmations in the morning

____

____

____

6 affirmations in the afternoon

____

____

____

____

____

9 affirmations in the evening

____

____

____

____

____

____

____

____

Today I am grateful for?

____

____

____

____

I want to manifest _______________________________
My affirmation:

3 affirmations in the morning

6 affirmations in the afternoon

9 affirmations in the evening

Today I am grateful for?

I want to manifest ____
My affirmation:

3 affirmations in the morning

____

____

____

6 affirmations in the afternoon

____

____

____

____

____

____

9 affirmations in the evening

____

____

____

____

____

____

____

____

____

Today I am grateful for?

____

____

____

____

I want to manifest ________________________________
My affirmation:

3 affirmations in the morning

____

____

____

6 affirmations in the afternoon

____

____

____

____

____

____

9 affirmations in the evening

____

____

____

____

____

____

____

____

____

Today I am grateful for?

____

____

____

____

____

I want to manifest ____
My affirmation:

3 affirmations in the morning

____

____

____

6 affirmations in the afternoon

____

____

____

____

____

____

9 affirmations in the evening

____

____

____

____

____

____

____

____

____

Today I am grateful for?

____

____

____

____

I want to manifest ___________________________
My affirmation:

3 affirmations in the morning

6 affirmations in the afternoon

9 affirmations in the evening

Today I am grateful for?

I want to manifest ______________________________________
My affirmation:

3 affirmations in the morning

____

____

6 affirmations in the afternoon

____

____

____

____

9 affirmations in the evening

____

____

____

____

____

____

____

Today I am grateful for?

____

____

____

____

I want to manifest __________________________________
My affirmation:

3 affirmations in the morning

6 affirmations in the afternoon

9 affirmations in the evening

Today I am grateful for?

I want to manifest ______________________________
My affirmation:

3 affirmations in the morning

____

____

____

6 affirmations in the afternoon

____

____

____

____

____

____

9 affirmations in the evening

____

____

____

____

____

____

____

____

____

Today I am grateful for?

____

____

____

____

____

I want to manifest ____
My affirmation:

3 affirmations in the morning

6 affirmations in the afternoon

9 affirmations in the evening

Today I am grateful for?

I want to manifest __________________________________
My affirmation:

3 affirmations in the morning

6 affirmations in the afternoon

9 affirmations in the evening

Today I am grateful for?

I want to manifest _______________________________________
My affirmation:

3 affirmations in the morning

6 affirmations in the afternoon

9 affirmations in the evening

Today I am grateful for?

I want to manifest ___________________________________
My affirmation:

3 affirmations in the morning

____

____

____

6 affirmations in the afternoon

____

____

____

____

____

9 affirmations in the evening

____

____

____

____

____

____

____

____

Today I am grateful for?

____

____

____

____

I want to manifest ___________________________________
My affirmation:

3 affirmations in the morning

____
____
____

6 affirmations in the afternoon

____
____
____
____
____
____

9 affirmations in the evening

____
____
____
____
____
____
____
____
____

Today I am grateful for?

____
____
____
____

I want to manifest ___________________________________
My affirmation:

3 affirmations in the morning

____

____

____

6 affirmations in the afternoon

____

____

____

____

____

____

9 affirmations in the evening

____

____

____

____

____

____

____

____

____

Today I am grateful for?

____

____

____

____

I want to manifest ___________________________________
My affirmation:

3 affirmations in the morning

____

____

____

6 affirmations in the afternoon

____

____

____

____

____

____

9 affirmations in the evening

____

____

____

____

____

____

____

____

____

Today I am grateful for?

____

____

____

____

I want to manifest ___________________________________
My affirmation:

3 affirmations in the morning

____

____

____

6 affirmations in the afternoon

____

____

____

____

____

____

9 affirmations in the evening

____

____

____

____

____

____

____

____

____

Today I am grateful for?

____

____

____

____

I want to manifest ___________________________________
My affirmation:

3 affirmations in the morning

____

____

____

6 affirmations in the afternoon

____

____

____

____

____

____

9 affirmations in the evening

____

____

____

____

____

____

____

____

____

Today I am grateful for?

____

____

____

____

I want to manifest _______________________________
My affirmation:

3 affirmations in the morning

6 affirmations in the afternoon

9 affirmations in the evening

Today I am grateful for?

I want to manifest ______________________________________
My affirmation:

3 affirmations in the morning

6 affirmations in the afternoon

9 affirmations in the evening

Today I am grateful for?

I want to manifest ________________________________
My affirmation:

3 affirmations in the morning

____

____

____

6 affirmations in the afternoon

____

____

____

____

____

____

9 affirmations in the evening

____

____

____

____

____

____

____

____

____

Today I am grateful for?

____

____

____

____

I want to manifest ______________________________
My affirmation:

3 affirmations in the morning

6 affirmations in the afternoon

9 affirmations in the evening

Today I am grateful for?

I want to manifest ____
My affirmation:

3 affirmations in the morning

____

____

____

6 affirmations in the afternoon

____

____

____

____

____

____

9 affirmations in the evening

____

____

____

____

____

____

____

____

____

Today I am grateful for?

____

____

____

____

I want to manifest ________________________
My affirmation:

3 affirmations in the morning

6 affirmations in the afternoon

9 affirmations in the evening

Today I am grateful for?

I want to manifest _____________________________
My affirmation:

3 affirmations in the morning

6 affirmations in the afternoon

9 affirmations in the evening

Today I am grateful for?

I want to manifest ______________________________
My affirmation:

3 affirmations in the morning

____

____

____

6 affirmations in the afternoon

____

____

____

____

____

____

9 affirmations in the evening

____

____

____

____

____

____

____

____

____

Today I am grateful for?

____

____

____

____

I want to manifest ____
My affirmation:

3 affirmations in the morning

____
____
____

6 affirmations in the afternoon

____
____
____
____
____
____

9 affirmations in the evening

____
____
____
____
____
____
____
____
____

Today I am grateful for?

____
____
____
____

I want to manifest __________________________
My affirmation:

3 affirmations in the morning

____

____

____

6 affirmations in the afternoon

____

____

____

____

____

____

9 affirmations in the evening

____

____

____

____

____

____

____

____

____

Today I am grateful for?

____

____

____

____

I want to manifest _______________________________
My affirmation:

3 affirmations in the morning

6 affirmations in the afternoon

9 affirmations in the evening

Today I am grateful for?

I want to manifest ____
My affirmation:

3 affirmations in the morning

6 affirmations in the afternoon

9 affirmations in the evening

Today I am grateful for?

I want to manifest _______________________________________
My affirmation:

3 affirmations in the morning

____

____

____

6 affirmations in the afternoon

____

____

____

____

____

____

9 affirmations in the evening

____

____

____

____

____

____

____

____

____

Today I am grateful for?

____

____

____

____

I want to manifest ____
My affirmation:

3 affirmations in the morning

____
____
____

6 affirmations in the afternoon

____
____
____
____
____
____

9 affirmations in the evening

____
____
____
____
____
____
____
____
____

Today I am grateful for?

____
____
____
____
____

I want to manifest _______________________________________
My affirmation:

3 affirmations in the morning

____
____
____

6 affirmations in the afternoon

____
____
____
____
____
____

9 affirmations in the evening

____
____
____
____
____
____
____
____
____

Today I am grateful for?

____
____
____
____

I want to manifest ____
My affirmation:

3 affirmations in the morning

____

____

____

6 affirmations in the afternoon

____

____

____

____

____

____

9 affirmations in the evening

____

____

____

____

____

____

____

____

____

Today I am grateful for?

____

____

____

____

I want to manifest ________________________________
My affirmation:

3 affirmations in the morning

____

____

____

6 affirmations in the afternoon

____

____

____

____

____

____

9 affirmations in the evening

____

____

____

____

____

____

____

____

____

Today I am grateful for?

____

____

____

____

I want to manifest _______________________________
My affirmation:

3 affirmations in the morning

____

____

____

6 affirmations in the afternoon

____

____

____

____

____

____

9 affirmations in the evening

____

____

____

____

____

____

____

____

____

Today I am grateful for?

____

____

____

____

I want to manifest ______________________________
My affirmation:

3 affirmations in the morning

____

____

____

6 affirmations in the afternoon

____

____

____

____

____

____

9 affirmations in the evening

____

____

____

____

____

____

____

____

____

Today I am grateful for?

____

____

____

____

I want to manifest ______________________________________
My affirmation:

3 affirmations in the morning

____

____

____

6 affirmations in the afternoon

____

____

____

____

____

____

9 affirmations in the evening

____

____

____

____

____

____

____

____

____

Today I am grateful for?

____

____

____

____

____

I want to manifest _______________________________________
My affirmation:

3 affirmations in the morning

6 affirmations in the afternoon

9 affirmations in the evening

Today I am grateful for?

I want to manifest _______________________________
My affirmation:

3 affirmations in the morning

____

____

____

6 affirmations in the afternoon

____

____

____

____

____

____

9 affirmations in the evening

____

____

____

____

____

____

____

____

____

Today I am grateful for?

____

____

____

____

I want to manifest _______________________________________
My affirmation:

3 affirmations in the morning

____

____

____

6 affirmations in the afternoon

____

____

____

____

____

____

9 affirmations in the evening

____

____

____

____

____

____

____

____

____

Today I am grateful for?

____

____

____

____